The World of Mary Jones

A Social History
of the people and places
that Mary knew.

by
Sara Eade

First published 2015

ISBN 978-0-9565652-7-3

Published by Sara Eade

saraeade@webleicester.co.uk

designed & printed by:

imprint

design & print

new road, newtown, powys, sy16 1bd

tel: (01686) 624137

sales@imprintnewtown.co.uk

Copyright

Please note that the spellings of towns have retained, as far as possible, the spelling used in Mary Jones' time.

The Imperial System

Measurement

1 inch or 1" = 25.4 mm

1 foot or 1' = 30.5 cm

1 yard = 0.914 m

There are 12 inches in a foot, 3 feet in a yard and a mile is 1760 yards = to 1.6093 km

220 yards = 1 Furlong and 10 chains = 1 Furlong

8 Furlongs = 1 mile

Area

1 acre (4840 sq yards) = 4064.86 m²

1 square mile (640 square yards) = 2.59 km²

1 perch = 5.5 yards

40 square perches - to 1 rood or rod

160 square perches to an acre

Rood is a surveying measurement

Liquid

1 pint = 0.55 litres

1 gallon = 4.55 litres

There are 8 pints in a gallon

Weight

1 ounce (1oz) = 28.35 g

1 pound (1lb) = 0.454 kg

1 stone (1st) = 6.35kg

1 quarter (1qt) = 12.70 kg

1 Hundredweight (1cwt) = 50.80 kg

1 ton (1t) = 1.01 Tonnes

There are 16ozs in a pound, 14 pounds in a stone, 2 stones in a quarter, 4 quarters in a hundredweight and 20 hundredweights in a ton.

Currency

12 pence (12d) make 1 shilling (1s) and, in turn 20 shillings make one pound (£1). At one time the sum of a 'guinea' was also used. A guinea was equal to 21 shillings.

One penny was subdivided into half pennies (1/2d) and farthings (1/4d)

In counting terms, a group of 12 was termed a dozen (1doz), 12 dozen made 1 gross.

Front Cover - Ceramic model of Mary Jones and the Bible in Llanfihangel y Pennant Church by Margaret Berry

FOREWORD

The lovely church of St Michael in Llanfihangel y Pennant, where Mary Jones was baptised, is still there today, a place of pilgrimage, captivating visitors from around the world with its simple beauty and with the story of Mary Jones, which is displayed in its vestry.

Still occasionally used for small-scale, intimate services, it is a place where people come to seek silence. It radiates a strong sense of the history of Christian witness in the valley, nowhere demonstrated more clearly than in the experience of Mary Jones. Her story is one that still excites and challenges people today.

Although many of us know the bare bones of the story of the young girl who set off across the hills, barefoot, to walk to Bala to buy a Welsh language Bible from the Reverend Thomas Charles, in fact most of us know little more than that.

In her book, "The World of Mary Jones" Sara Eade gives us a more complete story. Her extensive research has revealed a wealth of detail about Mary Jones' background, her surroundings, the society in which she lived, her family and the important people in her life.

The result is a book you can both dip into or read from cover to cover. Sara includes pictures of wonderful scenery, old photographs of the landscape and villages Mary Jones might have known, as well as letters and diaries from her time. In "The World of Mary Jones' we get to know her better than ever before.

Mary Jones' historic journey to buy a Welsh Bible was one of the factors leading to the establishment of the British and Foreign Bible Society. Now the Bible Society has created a new exhibition centre at St Beuno's Church, Llanycil, on the edge of Lake Bala, called "Mary Jones' World". It depicts the angle of the story based on the Reverend Thomas Charles.

However it is at St Michael's Church in Llanfihangel y Pennant where the Mary Jones story starts and the exhibition in the vestry, originally established by Margaret Lloyd Rees and updated in recent years by Sara Eade herself, continues to fascinate and delight people who have travelled from all over the world, as their comments in the visitor book testify.

Websites you might like to visit:

http://llanfihangel-y-pennant.org.uk

http://www.biblesociety.org.uk/about-bible-society/our-work/byd-mary-jones-world/

Reverend Richard A Vroom
Vicar of the Bro Ystumanner Ministry Area

DEDICATION

This book is dedicated to all those who have helped to preserve the memory of Mary Jones, not least of whom is Margaret Lloyd Rees who first put together a display of information about Mary and her family at St Michael's Church, Llanfihangel y Pennant. This display was updated in 2006 by Sara Eade, Irene Hale and Pauline Hey and with the help of the Peter Saunders Trust. It was updated again in 2015 with the help of The Bible Society.

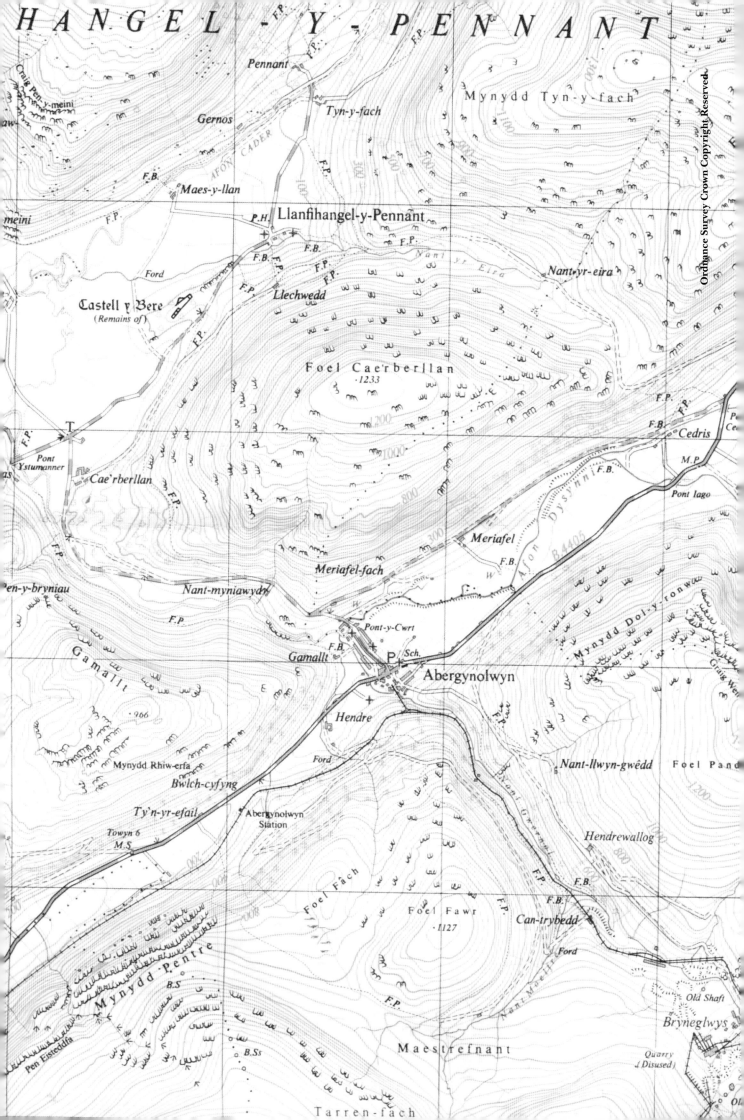

thanks

My thanks to the following people and places who have helped in the production of this book:

National Library of Wales, Merionethshire County Records Office at Dolgellau, Noel Williams, Martin Riley, Rev Richard Vroom, Margaret Lloyd Rees, Jane and Anthony Pearson, Buddug Thompson, Ian Walden, Richard Griffiths, David Hale, Irene Hale, Pauline Hey, Alastair Cooper, the Edwards' family from Bryncrug, Royston and Nia Jones, Arthur Davies and Eirlyr Jones.

Websites used include, Ancestry.com, Find My Past, Free BMD, Bible Society, Wikipedia etc

bibliography and references

The Life of Thomas Charles
by D E Jenkins

Great Britain Post Roads, Post Towns and Postal Rates 1635 – 1839
by Alan W Robertson

Echoes of Old Merioneth
by Hugh J Owen

From Merioneth to Botany Bay
by Hugh J Owen

Merionethshire Historical Society Journal 1990

Castell Y Bere leaflet
by C Graham Benham

Castell Y Bere leaflet
by Cadw

St Michael's Church leaflet
by Sara Eade

Bryneglwys Slate Quarry, Abergynolwyn
by Alan Holmes with Sara Eade

The Craft Industries
by Geraint Jenkins

Parish records for St Mary's Talyllyn, St Cadfan's , Tywyn, Llanfihangel y Pennant and Bethlehem Chapel, Bryncrug

INTRODUCTION

Over the years there have been lots of accounts written about Mary Jones and her historic walk to Bala in 1800 to buy a Bible which contributed to the formation of The British and Foreign Bible Society, now known as The Bible Society in 1804.

This is an attempt to record the story from a factual stance and as far as possible all the information comes from factual records of the time, together with known historical details about the area and its way of life.

Like any factually based piece of work, more information comes to light as soon as the work is published. If you have additional information about Mary Jones and/or her family and are willing to share it, please contact me at saraeade@webleicester.co.uk

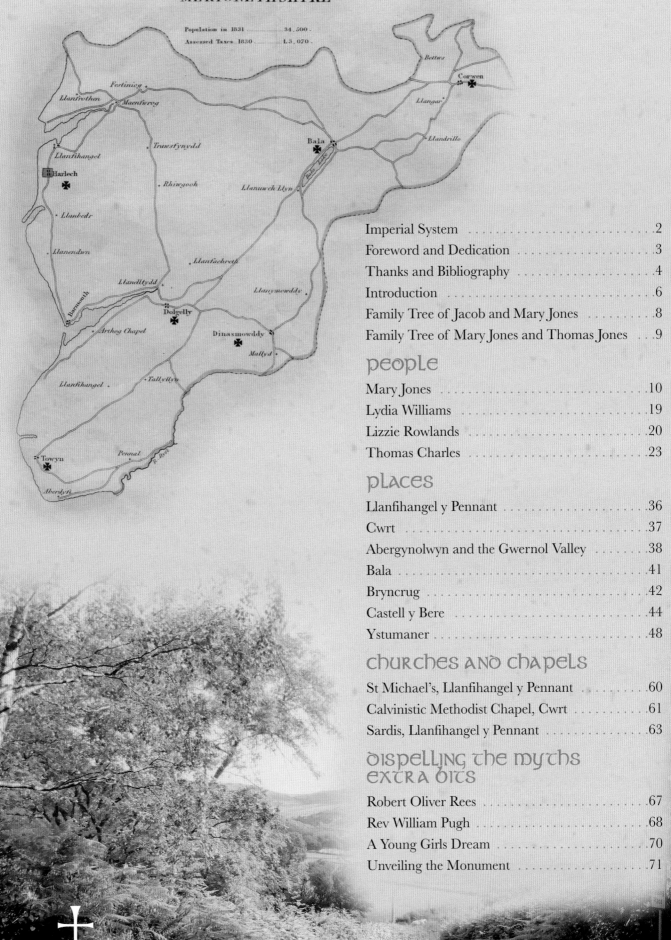

MERIONETHSHIRE

Population in 1831 . . . . . 34,500.
Assessed Taxes 1830 . . . . . L3,070.

Family lived at Tyn-y-Ddol, Llanfihangel y Pennant.
The family moved here shortlafter Mary was born.

Lewis Jones and Anne

Jacob Jones and Mary Jones

Bachelor

Spinster

Occupation: Peasant

Both made their mark X
in the register

Jacob Jones
Born C1758/9

Mary Jones (aka Molly)
Born C 1756/7

Witnesses: Edward Owen,
Mary Pugh

Died 16 4 1789
Llanfihangel y Pennant

Died 4 3 1837
Cwrt, Abergynolwyn

Register shows that Jacob
died from Asthma.
He was aged 30 years.

Married 25 5 1783 Llanfihangel y Pennant

After Mary died, her boidy
was taken to Llanfihangel
y Pennant where she was
buried with her husband
Jacob on the 3 7 1837.

Mary
Born 16 12 1784
Pen-y-Bryniau Mawr

Baptised 19 12 1784
Llanfihangel y Pennant

Mary was the couple's
only child

Family moved to Cwrt between 1813 and 1820
Family moved to Bryncrug in 1820
In 1841 Family were living at Pont Fathew, Bryncrug
In 1851 Mary was living in Bryncrug
In 1861 Mary was living at Pont Fathew, Bryncrug

Jacob Jones and Mary Jones

Lewis Jones and Anne

Mary Jones
Born 16 12 1784
Pen-y-Bryniau Mawr

Occupation: Weaver

Died 29 12 1864
Bryncrug
Mary died of old age

Thomas Jones
Baptised 25 12 1787
St Cadvan's Church, Towyn

Occupation: Plannel and Lynsey Weaver

Died 21 7 1849
Bryncrug
Thomas died from Tuburculosis

Married 27 2 1813 St Mary's Church, Talyllyn

The family were living at Minffordd Felindre
when the last three children were born

Lewis
Baptised 25 12 1813
Ll-y-P
Living at Cwrt
Abergynolwyn

Died 1831
Bryncrug
Aged 18 yrs
TB

Mary
Born 5 12 1815
Cwrt
Abergynolwyn
Baptised 24 12 1815
Cwrt
Abergynolwyn by
Robert Griffiths

Buried 27 8 1817
Ll-y-P
Family living at Cwrt
Abergynolwyn

Aged 2 years

Jacob
Born 22 2 1818
Cwrt
Abergynolwyn
Baptised 15 3 1818
Cwrt Abergynolwyn
by Robert Griffiths

Died 1833
Bryncrug

Aged 15 years
TB

Joan (John)
Born 24 7 1820
Bryncrug
Baptised 24 8 1820
Pen-y-Parc by
Robert Griffiths

Emigrated to USA
between 1841 and
1851

Ebenezer (Benny)
Born 12 9 1822
Bryncrug Baptised
19 10 1822
Bryncrug Chapel by
William Howard

Died young

Mary
Born 8 1 1826
Bryncrug
Baptised 29 1 1826
Bryncrug Chapel by
John Roberts

Died 1831
Bryncrug

Aged 5 years
TB

Llanfihangel y Pennant Church

Tyn y Ddol

Shortly after Mary was born, the family moved to a cottage called Tyn-y-Ddol in the hamlet of Tynyfach, about half a mile from the village of Llanfihangel y Pennant. The cottage was located next to a stream, which provided all the water the family needed. It was built from local stone and had a huge fireplace at one end. Beyond the wall with the fireplace in it was a room almost as big as the cottage and this was used to house the animals during the winter.

Pen-y-Bryniau Mawr and Llanfihangel y Pennant, nestle in the foothills of Cader Idris in Mid Wales. The parish of Llanfihangel y Pennant was quite a large one and covered the neighbouring hamlets of Cwrt and Pandy, later to become the village of Abergynolwyn. Hill farming was the main occupation and it was hard work as most of the land the farmers' worked was on a slope and prone to the severe weather experienced in the area. Wind was the main problem, as it was not only very strong but could be full of salt if it was coming in across the sea.

MARY JONES

was born on the 16th December 1784 at Pen-y-Bryniau Mawr to Jacob and Mary Jones who had been married on the 25th May 1783 at Llanfihangel y Pennant. In their marriage entry in the register, Jacob is described as a Peasant, which would have equated to an Agricultural Labourer today. The marriage was witnessed by Edward Owen and Mary Pugh. Neither Jacob, a bachelor nor Mary, a spinster, could write but they were both able to make their mark in the Register.

The grave of Jacob & Mary Jones

From a very early age Mary was expected to undertake chores around the house. Her father, Jacob, suffered with asthma and he died on the 16th April 1789 aged just 30. Mary was just 4 years and 4 months old. She and her mother continued to live at their cottage until the early 1800s when they moved to Cwrt, a hamlet near to the present day village of Abergynolwyn.

Mary's mother was a very religious woman and she and Mary were always seen at Chapel. They were members of the Calvinistic Methodist Church, which had originated in Wales in 1735-6, having been influenced by the travelling preachers who frequented the area. The nearest Calvinistic Methodist Chapel was at Cwrt, a good two miles away and each Sunday, Mary and her mother walked the distance meeting up with, and walking with friends.

Visiting preachers included the Rev Thomas Charles who was one of the prominent leaders of the Methodist Movement in Wales. He was born in 1755, brought up under the Methodist influence and attended Oxford University from 1775 to 1778 and was originally ordained into the Anglican Church.

Rev Thomas Charles settled in Bala in 1783 and was largely responsible for setting up a circulating Sunday School system in the area. Sunday schools provided people with the opportunity of learning to read and write and lessons were taken in the afternoon, between the morning and evening Chapel services. Those who had travelled a distance would take a meal of bread and cheese to eat at lunchtime.

Learning to read was important for all, as a week was a long time to wait to hear the next Bible story. The Rev Thomas Charles was also responsible for securing and distributing thousands of Welsh Bibles and it was he who encouraged Mary to save the money to buy her own Bible.

Rev. Thomas Charles

The nearest school was in Pandy run by a Mr Lewis Williams and Mary was still a pupil at the school when she walked to Bala to buy her Bible. Lewis Williams was from Llanfachreth near Dolgelley and he died on the 14th August 1862 aged 88.

By the time Mary was eight years old, she was beginning to learn to read and was offered the opportunity to read the Bible of Mr and Mrs Evans who had purchased a Bible some years earlier. On her day off, Mary used to walk the two miles to Mr and Mrs Evans' farm where she was allowed to sit in the parlour and read the Bible. By the time Mary was ten she had resolved to buy her own Bible and she started to undertake extra chores to earn the money she needed – 3s and 6d (17½p in today's money).

It took 6 years to save the money, earning it a little at a time. Mary kept a few chickens and sold the eggs and also kept extra hives of bees and sold the honey. She undertook some sewing work and was lucky enough to earn a whole sixpence when she retuned a wallet she had found, to its owner.

In 1864, a few months before she died Mary was interviewed by a Lizzie Jones, later Rowlands, who recorded Mary's own account, of her desire for a Bible and her journey to Bala:

Mary as a young girl, an illustration from the book by Mary E. Roper

Calvanistic Methodist Chapel at Cwrt, now two holiday cottages

Mary aged about 12 years in an illustration from the book by Mary E Roper

'One stormy Monday morning I was walking to a farmhouse about two miles from my home, a gentleman riding a white horse and wearing a cloth cape came to meet me and asked where I was going through such wind and rain. I said I was going to a farmhouse where there was a Bible, that there wasn't one nearer my home and that the mistress of the farm had said that I could see the Bible which she kept on a table in the parlour as long as I took my clogs off. I told him that I was saving every half penny, this long time, to get a Bible but that I did not know where I could get one. The gentleman was Charles of Bala. He told me to come to Bala at a certain time, that he was expecting some Bibles from London and that I could have one from him.

When the time came, my mother put the money and a little bread and cheese in one end of a wallet and my clogs in the other, and I set off for Bala on a fine morning resting where there was a stream of clear water to eat the bread and cheese. I came to Bala and trembling, knocked the door of Mr Charles' house. I asked for Mr Charles and was told he was in his study at the back of the house. I was allowed to go to him and he told me the Bibles had not arrived. I started to cry because I did not know where to stay. He sent me to an old servant of his who had a house at the bottom of the garden, until the Bibles came. When they came, Mr Charles gave me three for the money that is for the price of one. I set off home with my precious burden. I ran a great part of the way, I was so glad of my Bible.'

Mr Charles, House in Bala, an illustration from the book by Mary E Roper

Mary ready for the trip to Bala, an illustration from the book by Mary E Roper

Lizzie Rowlands, a native of Bala came to Bryncrug in 1862 as a Governess to the children of Griffith and Elizabeth Jones of Gwyddelfynedd Farm. On hearing that there was a young woman from Bala in the village, Mary asked her to call and a friendship was struck up. Lizzie called to see Mary several times a week and she read the Bible to Mary on many occasions.

Mary's endeavour added to the Rev Thomas Charles' desire to make Bibles accessible to all and led him and others to set up the British and Foreign Bible Society in 1804. The organisation raised funds to print Bibles and to send them all around the world and for anyone who wanted one. Mary had made the journey to Bala in 1800 when she was 15 years old.

St Mary's Church, Talyllyn

Sara Eade

Cwrt Abergynolwyn

A cottage in Cwrt similar to that which Mary & Thomas & Family lived in

Sara Eade Collection

Inside St Mary's Church, Talyllin

Very little is known about Mary's life from then on until 1813 except that she lived with her mother in Cwrt. On the 27th February 1813, Mary married Thomas Jones at St Mary's Church, Talyllyn. The entry in the register reads:

'Thomas Jones of the Parish of Towyn, Bachelor, and Mary Jones of this Parish, Spinster, were married in this church by banns with consent of parents this 27th day of February 1813.'

Both signed their names and the witnesses were Ann Jones and Lewis Jones.

Thomas Jones' parents were Lewis and Anne Jones and Thomas was baptised at St Cadfan's Church, in Towyn on 25th December 1787.

Thomas and Mary's first child, Lewis, was born in December and baptised on 25th December 1813 at Llanfihangel y Pennant. The baptismal record shows the family were living in Cwrt, Abergynolwyn and that Thomas was a Labourer.

Following the birth of Lewis was Mary and Thomas' second child Mary, who was born on 5th December 1815 at Cwrt, Abergynolwyn. She was baptised on 24th December 1815 at the Calvinistic Methodist Chapel at Cwrt by Robert Griffiths. She sadly died before she reached her second birthday and was buried at Llanfihangel y Pennant on the 17th August 1817 aged 1 year. The Burial Register records that the family were living at Cwrt, Abergynolwyn.

Their third child, Jacob was born on the 22nd February 1818 at Cwrt, Abergynolwyn, and he was baptised on the 15th March 1818 at the Calvinistic Methodist Chapel at Cwrt by Robert Griffiths. The Chapel was founded around 1797 and the first baptisms to take place were in December 1815. The entries show that Mary was entry number 2 and Jacob entry number 5. The Chapel's Baptismal Register ends in 1837, the last baptism took place on 9th April 1837. A total of 39 baptisms had taken place. For both Mary and Jacob, their father, Thomas' occupation is given as that of a Labourer.

Sometime in the first half of 1820, the family moved to Bryncrug where their fourth child John (entered as Joan in the register) was born on the 24th July 1820. The Calvinistic Methodist Baptismal Register for The Bethlehem Chapel recorded a great deal of information including the fact the Thomas was a Weaver and that the family were living at Minffordd Felindre. John was baptised on the 24th August 1820 at Pen-y-Parc by Robert Griffiths.

It is not known why the family moved but Thomas did come from Bryncrug and he was an Elder of the Calvinistic Methodist Chapel and may have moved to help run the Bethlehem. The Chapel was founded around 1800 and the first baptism is recorded as having taken place on September 19th 1808. The last baptism in this register took place on 11th October 1836. A total of 42 baptisms had taken place.

Ebenezer was their fifth child and was born on 12th September 1822 at Bryncrug. He was baptised on the 19th October 1822 at The Bethlehem Chapel in Bryncrug by William Howard. Nothing else is known about Ebenezer other than he was probably known as Benny and died from Tuberculosis at a very young age.

Thomas and Mary's last child was Mary born on the 8th January 1826 at Bryncrug and baptised on the 29th January 1826 by John Roberts. Sadly Mary did not survive long and died, aged 5 years in 1831 having suffered from Tuberculosis.

Sheep Shearing

Bryncrug

Tuberculosis was also the cause of the deaths of Lewis who died in 1831 aged 18 years and Jacob who died in 1833 aged 15 years.

The surviving son did not contract Tuberculosis and appears on the 1841 census aged 20, living at home with Thomas aged 50 and Mary aged 55 at Pont Fathew, which is the part of Bryncrug around the river and the cottages along the road out of the village towards Llanegryn.

In Bryncrug, as in Cwrt, Abergynolwyn, the woollen industry was one of the main sources of employment. Many people were home weavers. The hills around were the homes of sheep farming with the Welsh Mountain sheep being the main breed. Some farms kept a few Jacob sheep and it is believed that goats were also kept. Many people have seen wild goats on Bird Rock, the remnants of escaped domestic goats, left to fend for themselves.

If the raw wool is to be spun into an even yarn, it has to be sorted. The fibres from one single fleece vary greatly. Skilled wool sorters will unroll a fleece and separate off as many as ten or eleven different qualities, the finest of which comes from the wool, which grows around the shoulders and sides whilst the coarsest comes from the belly, legs and throat.

The fleece is then scoured – washed to remove the dirt and grease or lanolin, this process is necessary if dyeing is to take place before weaving, so that the dye will take. In older times, the wool was washed to remove the dirt but the lanolin was left in as it was felt to aid the spinning process.

Dyeing can take place at three stages during the making of a cloth. Firstly the fleece can be dyed before spinning. When this is done, coloured fleece can be blended together to make vibrant, soft or rich tones. Secondly the spun yarn can be dyed before being woven and thirdly the woven cloth can be dyed as a whole piece.

After scouring and dyeing comes willeying where the fleece is opened up and disentangled before spinning. This process was also known as willowing, as before the eighteenth century, the sticks used to beat the fleece were cut from willow trees. During this process, vegetable oil can be added to the wool fibres to lubricate them.

Carding the fibres is the most important stage before spinning. This lines all the fibres up so that the can be spun together. Carding frames were made with rows of teasel heads in times gone by and these were also grown locally.

Bryncrug Village

Spinning the fibres created the thread, which was then woven into different lengths of cloth. In Mary's day, spinning took place in homes too, and the finished thread would be delivered to the weavers to make up. Spinning was a hard task and many welsh homes had a simple spinning wheel on the go from morning until night in a corner of the kitchen and it was not unusual to see even small children taking their turn.

Weaving was done on small wooden frames with a fixed width of cloth. We can only imagine that Mary and Thomas were weaving simple Welsh flannel, which after fulling, would have been made up into whatever was required locally and sold locally.

Mary's death certificate tells us that Thomas was a Linsey and Flannel Weaver.

Linsey was a finely woven cloth in a plain weave (one over one) fabric in which the warp threads – those going from top to bottom were made from linen or tow, which was the shorter fibres from flax, hemp, ramie or jute, and the weft threads – those on the bobbin going from left to right – in wool. Linsey, being a light-weight fabric, was ideal for clothing and was also used to produce light blankets as well as top coverings for beds. It could also be quilted.

By the time the 1851 census was taken, Mary had lost both her husband and her son. She is listed as a Widow, aged 66 years and her occupation is given as a Weaver. Thomas had died on the 21st July 1849 in Bryncrug and his death certificate gives the cause of death as consumption (tuberculosis).

Prosbyterain Church in Brynant, this building built in 1883 replaced the one which Mary attended

Lizzie Rowlands tells us that John emigrated to America and as he is not listed on the 1851 census so we have to assume that he went to America sometime between 1841 and 1851. Whether he went before his father died or not, we may never know. Lizzie also records that John sent letters from America to his mother, which Lizzie read to her. Lizzie, herself also wrote to John. As Lizzie started to visit Mary from September 1862 until Mary died in December 1864, John was alive but as yet no record of him has been found.

This period in the history of the local area is a significant one. The Corn Laws were repealed in 1846 having been brought in, in 1815, following the Napoleonic wars when the agricultural industry was in a severe depression. The Corn Law prevented the import of wheat unless the price of British grain rose to £4.00 a quarter. To a degree the law was a success as it did help to protect British farming from foreign competition. The Corn Law however, pushed the price of bread beyond the means of many people, which caused great distress to the poor.

The Anti-Corn Law League was formed in 1838 to campaign for the repeal of the laws. In west Merionethshire, the damage was already beginning as the prices of bread remained high and people began to starve. In the early 1840s this coincided with some devastating harvests and food was hard to come by.

The situation was rescued by Richard Pryce of Dolaugwyn who took matters into his own hands and went to Liverpool where he bought two ships of wheat and brought them back to Towyn to feed the hungry of the town and the surrounding area. Richard Parry of Bryncrug composed a song in Richard's honour.

Dolaugwyn

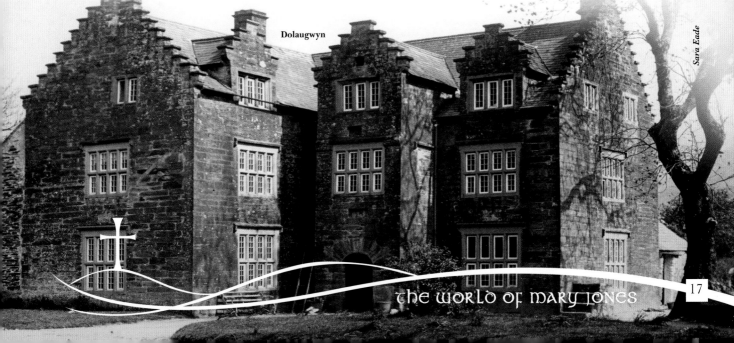

The original song was written in Welsh and is roughly translated as:

"There is a special person
Living over at Dolaugwyn.
He went away to Liverpool
To buy corn and flour
And the main purpose was
To keep the poor alive.
He filled a ship with food
And Nature gave the wind
To fill her sails,
And bring her home
across the waves.
To the Pryces, and their
worthy family
Lovable as be they all
'I wish them every success
Whilst they of this world are'"

Whether or not Richard gave the grain away or sold it, it is not known but the famine might be a clue as to why Mary's only remaining child went to America. At the time America was seen as, the Promised Land, where food and work were freely available and Mary may have felt that this was the best thing for him to do. Maybe the lack of food contributed to Thomas' failing health and Richard's grain arrived too late to make a difference – we shall never know.

There were two Corn Mills in the area, one at Maes y Pandy between Talyllyn Lake and Abergynolwyn and the other at Felin Caerberllan which was on the road from Cwrt to Llanfihangel y Pennant. Sadly neither of the mills is in operation today.

The last miller at Maes y Pandy was Dafydd Davis and he worked there until about 1885. The mill at Maes y Pandy could process oats as well as corn and there was a kiln on the farm which was used to bake the oats before milling. In those days the baker was the person who baked the oats !

Mary lived on, gradually going blind, and again Lizzie Rowland gives us an insight as to Mary's life at that time:

'She (Mary Jones), was nearly 80 years old, small, thin, with a melancholy ungrateful expression and quite blind these many years, living in a small, miserable cottage. The poorest I have ever been in with an earthen floor, a small table with a rush candle on it and two or three three-legged stools. She wore the old Welsh dress, a petticoat and bed gown, an apron made of linsey and a white cap with a pleat on the side of her mouth. To go out to Chapel, she would wear a 'Jim Crow' (a soft felt hat), a blue homespun cloak and a hood and carry a stick in her hand.
In winter she used to carry a lantern with horn windows, not to light her way, she could not see, but so others could see her.'

Mary died on the 29th December 1864 and is buried in the graveyard attached to the Bethlehem Chapel in Bryncrug. Her death certificate gives the cause of death as simply 'old age' and records that she was the widow of Thomas Jones, Linsey and Flannel Weaver. Sadly no obituary in any of the local papers has been found.

Mary Jones' grave in Bryncrug

So what happened to the Bibles?

There were three altogether and as far as we know, the one that Mary herself used is in the Cambridge University Library. It had been published in 1799. On the fly-leaf and in Mary's own hand, is the following inscription:

'Mary Jones was
Born 16th December 1784
I bought this in the 16 year
of my age. I am daughter
of Jacob Jones and Mary Jones
his wife. The Lord may
give me grace today.
Mary Jones This the True
Owner of this Bible
Bought in the Year
1800 Age 16'

The home Mary lived in, in Bryncrup, until her campanion Lydia Williams died

Another is at The National Library of Wales, at Aberystwyth. This is the Bible which was used by Mary's Aunt, Ann Richards and written on the inside cover are the following words:

'Ann Richard
Her Bible
When I am dead and in my grave
with all my bones
In this book you shall see my name
then I shall not be forgotten.'

Also glued into this Bible is an envelope with the name Lydia's Bible written on it and inside is a paper written in Welsh. Lydia Williams lived with Mary during the last years of her life in the cottage at Bryncrug.

The third we can only assume was taken by John to America, a very special gift from his mother to remind him of home and to provide inspiration in his life.

Research into the Bibles was undertaken in 1885 and the researcher wrote to Elizabeth Jones of Gwyddfynyd Farm at Bryncrug. The letter does not now exist but the reply was as follows:

'Gwyddfynyd Oct 26th 1885
Dear Friend
In answer to your letter I beg to give you all the information I have been able to get concerning the other bible Mary Jones brought from Bala.
She brought it for her Aunt, cousin to her mother named Anne Richard Tynyr eithiw near Bryncrug where she died. At her death her son had it who married a daughter of the old preacher William Pugh Cwrt Abergynolwyn. There (sic) daughter Lydia Williams lived at Bryncrug and I saw the bible in her possession. She gave it to our governess Miss Jones now Mrs Rowlands Board School Penrhyndeudraeth who has it still at least had it when I saw her last. It was no trouble at all to me to

gain the information. Should you require any other information I shall be glad to help you.
With best respects
Yours Truly
Elizabeth Jones'

Mary's mother lived until she was 80 and died on the 4th March 1837. She had continued to live in Cwrt but after she died, was taken over to Llanfihangel y Pennant where she was buried with her husband Jacob on the 3rd July 1837. Their grave reads as follows:

'HERE
Lie the body of Jacob Jones
Who died April 16th 1789
Aged 30
Also the remains of Mary
His wife who died March
4th 1837 aged 80 years'

Steps on the outside of Tyn y Ddol

Did Mary know what her walk to Bala had started? The answer to this question is probably not to start with, though she would have known of The British and Foreign Bible Society. The Rev Thomas Charles continued his work until 1814 when he died. By then The British and Foreign Bible Society had been in existence for 10 years. In that time a great many Bibles had been printed and distributed in a wide variety of languages all over the world. The Bible Society continues that work today.

Mary's epic journey is commemorated in two places for all to see. Two monuments were erected, one in the middle of the ruins of Tyn-y-Ddol which reads:

IN MEMORY OF MARY JONES,
WHO IN
THE YEAR 1800, AT THE AGE OF
16 WALKED
FROM HERE TO BALA TO
PROCURE FROM THE
REV THOMAS CHARLES BA
A COPY OF THE WELSH BIBLE,
THIS INCIDENT
WAS THE OCCASION OF THE
FORMATION OF
THE BRITISH AND FOREIGN
BIBLE SOCIETY
ERECTED BY THE SUNDAY
SCHOOLS OF MERIONETH

Mary's Monument at Tyn y Ddol

Sara Eade

and the other in the graveyard at The Bethlehem Calvinistic Methodist Chapel in Bryncrug. The latter reads as follows:

'IN MEMORY OF
MARY JONES
WHO IN THE YEAR 1800
AT THE AGE OF 16,
WALKED FROM
LLANFIHANGEL Y PENNANT
TO BALA
TO PROCURE A COPY OF A
WELSH BIBLE FROM THE
REV THOMAS CHARLES, BA
THIS INCIDENT LED TO THE
FORMATION
OF THE BRITISH AND FOREIGN
BIBLE SOCIETY'

There is no plaque on Mary's house in Bryncrug, but ask anyone who lives in the village and they will tell you – it's the last cottage on the left as you leave the village for Llanegryn. Looking at it today it is hard to imagine that there was enough light coming through the small windows to enable weaving to take place. Candles would not give enough light and were to be used sparingly as even the

locally made reed candles were expensive to produce. One can only assume that once learnt, it was the sort of activity undertaken more by touch than anything else.

It was a hard life yet Mary still managed to live until she was 80 years of age and she left behind the legacy that shows that one person can make a difference and that, that one person does not have to rich or be in a privileged position or live in a big city.

A young girl just walked to Bala to buy a Bible...

Mary Jones' Memorial in Bryncrug

Mary Jones as she might have been on her walk, an illustration from the book by Robert Oliver Rees

Mary Jones' Home

Sara Eade Collection

Lydia Williams was born in 1815/6 in Llanfihangel y Pennant the daughter of Lewis Williams and it is believed, Lowry Pugh, the daughter of the Rev William Pugh who had been the Curate at Llanfihangel y Pennant in the 1790s.

In the 1841 census Lydia was living at Peniarth with Evan Rowlands, a Farmer. Lydia was aged 25 and a Farm Servant. By 1851, Lydia had moved to Bertheitiau and was visiting with Gwen Williams, an unmarried lady aged 73, and possibly a relative on her father's side.

By 1861, Lydia was living with Mary Jones in a cottage in Bryncrug described as 'opposite Gwydy'. Lydia was aged 46 and described as an 'Almswoman formerly House Servant', whilst Mary Jones was aged 73, a Widow and described as an 'Almswoman formerly an Agricultural Labourer'.

Lizzie Rowlands, who visited Mary and Lydia between September 1862 and Lydia's death in the autumn of 1864, described Lydia thus:

> *'She was truly good, pious, and amiable and cheerful in the greatest poverty and ill health.'*

> *'She (Mary Jones) was not a favourite with anyone. Lydia was a different person. She was a dear creature – so sweet and saintly.'*

Lydia died aged just 49 in the autumn of 1864 in Bryncrug.

Sara Eade

Bryncrug Village

Sara Eade

Sara Eade Collection

Lizzie Rowlands was born Elizabeth Jones in 1840/41 in Chester, the daughter of Elizabeth Jones. Lizzie had two brothers, James Davis born in 1852/3 and Goronwy. Little is known about Lizzie's parents as by 1871 her mother was aged 54, a Widow and she had formerly been a Shopkeeper.

Lizzie must have received a good education because in September 1862, aged 21, she arrived at Gwyddfynyd Farm in Bryncrug as a Governess to the children of Griffith and Elizabeth Jones. Griffith was the son of Richard Jones, Wern, and father of Mrs Richard Humphreys Morgan of Towyn. At that time, Gwyddfynyd Farm was a large farm and the family were considered 'well to do'.

Lizzie remained their Governess until the autumn of 1865, when she left her post to take up a similar post at Fael Dref.

Lizzie married Lewis Jones in the autumn of 1866. Lewis was the son of Laura Jones and was born in Llanddwyn in 1836/7. He trained as a Schoolmaster but sadly by the time the 1871 census was taken Lewis had died aged just 34. Lizzie together with her two sons was living at the British School House in Llanddwyn.

The couple had two sons, John Llewelyn born in the autumn of 1867 and Ieuen Robert born in the winter of 1869.

In the summer of 1873 and in Oswestry, Lizzie married Robert Rowlands, who was born in 1839/40 in Llanberis, Carnarvonshire. Robert was a Schoolmaster. The couple then had a daughter, Margaret in the summer of 1876 in Bala.

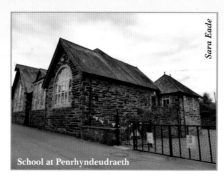
School at Penrhyndeudraeth

By the time the 1881 census was taken the family had settled at the Board School House at Llanfihangel y Traethau, Merionethshire with Robert aged 41 and a certified Teacher, Lizzie aged 40 and John Llewelyn aged 13, Ieuen Robert 11 and Margaret 4.

By 1891 the family had moved to Penrhyndeudraeth where they were living in the Board School House. Robert is the certified Schoolmaster aged 51 with Lizzie aged 50 and also a certified Schoolmistress. John Llewelyn is aged 23 and has trained as a Teacher and is listed as a certified Master, Ieuen Robert is aged 21 and is an Assistant Master and Margaret who would have been 14 is not at home, so it is possible that she is at a school away from home.

The couple stay at Penrhyndeudraeth for some time as the 1901 census sees them still living at the Board School House with Robert still teaching and aged 61. Lizzie is aged 60 and probably retired as no occupation is listed for her. All three children are now living away from home.

By 1911 Robert has retired and is aged 71. He is staying with Henry and Dora Hughes at Islwyn, Cynfal, Corwen.

Lizzie died in the spring of 1916 in Corwen aged 75.

Rev David E Jenkins interviewed Lizzie towards the end of her life:

'I interviewed Mrs Rowlands, Y Wern, Llandrillo, on Friday, October 21 1910. I took the 8.30 am train from Denbigh to Corwen, and cycled from there on, reaching Y Wern about 10.20. I passed through Cynwyd during the rain, and the road was very heavy and dirty. Mr Rowlands met me at the door of his house, and after showing me to a seat in the front room, went to assist Mrs Rowlands to get ready for the pre-arranged interview. While Mrs Rowlands was being removed from her bedroom to the room in which I sat, Mr Rowlands took me to the old bridge over the parapet of which Mrs Charles and her son were thrown in an accident. The old bridge is only a part of the present bridge – the part next Y Wern. It remains intact, as one can see without difficulty. The irregularity of the arch contrasts with the well-wrought new portion.

On our way back to the house, Mr Rowlands went into the day school of the village, and called out the master, who is a son of Mrs Rowlands by a previous marriage; and Mr and Mrs Rowlands live with him. He lost no time in making known to me his annoyance because the MSS about

Penrhyndeudraeth School

which I had come to interview his mother had been sent on to me, since he had some intention of using his mother's account of Mary Jones and her walk to Bala for some purpose of his own. He gave me to understand also that he was not willing that I should in any way make use of them just now. I replied that I had no desire to infringe his rights, or to bring pressure, even, for his consent. His wishes would be respected by me as far as the MSS was concerned. But I pointed out to him that their value was far less than he thought apart from the documents published in the life of Charles. Her story differed from Robert Oliver Rees's, and standing alone and apart, it was only a question of Mrs Rowlands' word against that of the gentleman referred to. I asked him to think the matter over, and to give me his decision after I had seen his mother. He returned to the school and I followed Mr Rowlands into the house, where I now saw Mrs R for the first time, though we had lived as all but neighbours, when she was at Penrhyn Deudraeth and I was at Portmadoc, seven years.

Mrs R sat with her back to the corner of the room, facing the centre of the room, and gave me a very warm welcome, though that could not be shown in the handshake, because of her old enemy, rheumatism. She has the features of her family, one characteristic of which is intelligence. She was very grey, all but toothless, I should imagine from the shape of her face. After a few preliminary remarks and inquiries, she gave me the following account of her connection with the transfer of Mary Jones's Bible from Robert Oliver Rees to the Library of Bala College. I am giving this record from notes which I took down at the time, supplemented by my memory.

"After I married Mr Rowlands I returned to my native town, Bala, where Mr Rowlands was master of the day-school. When a child, I used to play with the children of the late Dr Lewis Edwards – we lived next door but one to his house, the Saundersons were living between us. Mrs Edwards was always very partial to me, and after my return to Bala, she invited me up to the College house to tea – they were living at the College at this time. After tea, and while Mrs Edwards was doing something she had to attend to, I said 'I am going to the Library for a short time now'; and I ran up the stairs into the Library, and asked old Evan Owen, the librarian, to show me to Mary Jones's Bible. Evan Owen was a little man, and as cantankerous as any man I have ever known. He snapped at me with the question, 'What Mary Jones? What Bible?' 'I thought he was trying to put me off, and so I spoke a bit sharp to him back. We both got heated, and when I found that he would not give me any information, I ran back to Mrs Edwards, quite excited. I told her, as best as I could, what had passed between Evan Owen and myself, and I then found she knew nothing about Mary Jones or her Bible. She told Dr Edwards what I said, and then he wanted to know the whole story. His utter ignorance of the whole matter threw some light on the conduct of Evan Owen, and I told him that Mary Jones had been to Bala to get Bibles from Mr Charles, that the copy she had kept for herself had passed into the hands of Robert Griffith, Bryncrug, and that he had given it to Robert Oliver Rees to be repaired and handed over to the College. He then asked when the Bible had passed to Mr Rees's keeping, and I said that it was more than five years since. He had never heard a word of Mary Jones or her Bible, much less of the gift.

Mary Jones in her later years, the controversial drawing which Lizzie didn't like

Sara Eade Collection

Dr Edwards wrote, without delay, to demand the Bible, and it was sent on soon afterwards. To prove to you that Robert Oliver Rees knew that Mary Jones had received more than one Bible from Mr Charles, he sent to me, some time after this, to ask me to have Lydia's copy to repair. I wrote him a stinging letter in reply, calling his attention to the falsehoods he had written in his "Mari Jones a'I Beibl". I showed the letter to Dr Edwards and to Dr Parry before sending it, and they approved of it. Indeed they did was tantamount to encouraging it, because they thought that the story written by him was not only too sentimental, but unjust to Mr Charles. I got no reply from him, and, not long afterwards, he died. Dr Edwards used to tease me that I had killed him.

Among other things, I called him to account for putting in his book, as the portrait of Mary Jones, that of an old woman from Dolgelley, dressed up for the occasion and to deceive people. I wish I could draw. The face and general appearance of Mary Jones are as vivid to me to-day as they were on the day I last saw her alive. She must have been a fine, strong woman in her day; but, when I knew her, she was thin and shrunken. Her features had become somewhat small, her disposition was not at all a nice one. She was cross and peevish, until sometimes one felt like giving her a good talking to. She was not a favourite with anyone. Lydia was a different person. She was a dear creature – so sweet and saintly.

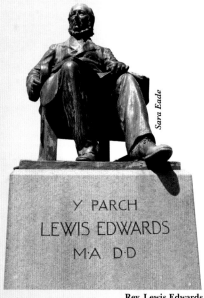

Y PARCH
LEWIS EDWARDS
M·A D·D

Sara Eade

Rev. Lewis Edwards

When the Bible Society sent to ask for Mary Jones's Bible, Dr Edwards persuaded his Committee to let them have it, because he could get the copy which Lydia gave me to replace it. If it were not for my copy, the Bible Society would never have been given the Bible, now in the Bible House. It was at that time that Robert Oliver Rees wrote to ask me to let him have my copy to repair before it was handed over to the College. I told him that my Bible would not pass from my hands to anyone except to Dr Edwards. I was so friendly with him and Mrs Edwards that I could not refuse it."

Then Mr Ieuan R Jones came in, and told me how the college people had allowed his mother's copy to be huddled up with other old books, and could not say which was the copy until his mother went to point it out to them. With this, Mrs Rowlands showed me a letter from the late Principal Edwards, asking her to go to Bala to identify the Bible she had given to his father. The letter was in the handwriting of Miss Marian Edwards, now Mrs Treborth Jones, Cardiff, but signed by the dear old Principal himself.

I next asked Mr Ieuan R Jones if he had made up his mind as to whether he would let me use the facts which his mother had given me; but he still seemed unwilling. However, after showing him the few facts I required to use in the Preface to the second edition of the Life of Charles would not

depreciate the value of the MSS, he gave his consent. I understood to limit my use of them to the substance only. I have strictly adhered to this undertaking in the materials which I went to the press, October 22, 1910.

After partaking of a cup of tea kindly prepared for me, I mounted my bicycle again at 12:7 pm, and rode back to Corwen, to catch the 1:15 train. Before I reached Cynwyd, the chain of the bicycle (borrowed), which was much too tight, snapped. I walked on hurriedly, cycling down the hills, and caught my train in good time.

Typed on Tuesday, October 25, 1910

D E Jenkins'

Lizzie had written a note relating to the donation of Lydia Williams' Bible to The Calvinistic Methodist College in Bala. The original was in Welsh and a translation is:

'This is the Bible of Lydia Williams, the niece of Mary Jones who lived with her but died before her. On her death bed Lydia gave me the Bible, which was one of three given to Mary Jones by The Reverend Charles. When the college released Mary's Bible to The Bible House, Dr Lewis Edwards knew where this Bible was kept. When on an engagement at Penrhyndeudraeth he called at my house and who was I not to place it in his sacred Hands. Happily yet profound I presented it to him.

Lizzie Rowlands, Council School, Penrhyndeudraeth'

Bala College

Sara Eade

Rev Thomas Charles.
(from a Gospel magazine 1797)

Thomas Charles was born on the 14th October 1755 and baptised on the 26th October 1755 at Longmoor, Abercywyn in Carmarthenshire. He was the son of Rees Charles and his second wife, Jael Bowen, who were married on the 19th December 1743. The couple had at least eleven children, Jane, David, Jael, Thomas, Elizabeth, Rees, Ann, David, John, Rees and Charlotte. Both the early David and Rees died young. Rees Charles had first married Jane Thomas on the 12th December 1738 at Llangunnor and the couple had two children, William and Sage before Jane died between 1742 and 1743.

Thomas Charles married Sarah Jones (known as Sally), who was the daughter of David and Jane Jones and who was born on the 12th November 1753 in Bala. Sally's father was a shopkeeper in Bala and after her father died; she carried on the family business which later helped to finance the work which Thomas Charles undertook in promoting the Christian message and in setting up his circulating Sunday Schools.

The couple were married on the 20th August 1783 at Llanycil Church, just outside the town of Bala and on the edge of the lake Llyn Tegid. This church building is now the home of 'Mary Jones World' which was opened in October 2014.

The couple had three children. The first was Thomas Rice Charles baptised at Llanycil on the 6th June 1785. Sally refers to their firstborn in a letter she wrote to her husband on the 18th June 1785:

'I am in our room hearing Gwen Singing for little Tomy who is sleeping Sweetly.'

Thomas went on to run the family business after his mother died. He married Maria Jones, the daughter of William and Elizabeth Jones, on the 22nd December 1806. Maria was born on the 26th February 1785 in Wrexham. Her father's occupation was a Saddler.

Thomas and Maria had five children, Sarah born in 1807, Maria in 1809, Thomas in 1810, David in 1812 and Jane in 1813. Thomas died, aged just 33 and was buried at Llanycil on the 1st February 1819. He shares a grave memorial with his sister Sarah, brother

David Jones, wife Maria and daughter Maria which reads:

'Also of Thomas Rice Charles, eldest son of the Rev Thomas Charles. He died in the year 1819 aged 34 years. Also of David Jones Charles younger son of the Rev Thomas Charles. He died in the year 1821 aged 28 years. Also of Maria daughter of the above Thomas Rice Charles and wife of Dr Owen Richards of Bala. She died in February 1836 aged 27 years. Also of Maria, Relict of the above Thomas Rice Charles. She died in 1852 aged 67.'

Sarah was born on the 15th September 1807 in Bala and was baptised on the 21st October 1807 at St Peter's Church in Liverpool. She married a cousin, David Charles on the 1st February 1832 at Llanycil. The marriage was witnessed by George Phillips and Maria Charles. Sarah's husband was a Calvinistic Methodist Minister and the family went to live at Ulverston in Cumbria.

David went on to become a Calvinistic Methodist Minister after being educated at Bala, Chirk and Jesus College, Oxford. He and his brother in law, Lewis Edwards (husband of his sister Jane) were involved with the inception of a preparatory school at Bala which later became the Calvinistic Methodist Theological College. In 1868 he undertook organising work in conjunction with a new University at Aberystwyth which was opened in 1872. When his nephew, Thomas Charles Edwards was appointed Principal of the

Llanycil Church

Bala High Street

The Lychgate at Llanycil Church

Lewis Edwards

Thomas Charles Edwards, First Principal of Aberystwyth University.

University, David Charles resigned his post and retired to Aberdovey where he died on the 13th December 1879. He was buried in Llanidloes.

David Charles married twice, first to Kate Roberts in 1839, and after she died in 1844, he married Mary Watkins, the widow of Benjamin Watkins, in 1846, with whom he had three daughters. Sadly two of his daughters pre-deceased him.

Maria married Owen Richards on the 2nd March 1835 at Llanycil and the marriage was witnessed by David Charles and Jane Charles. Sadly Maria died in February 1836 and was buried at Llanycil on the 6th February 1836.

Jane married Lewis Edwards at Llanycil on the 30th December 1836 and the marriage was witnessed by Thomas Edwards and Jane Roberts. Lewis became the Principal at the Calvinistic Methodist College in Bala and he and his wife were close friends of Lizzie Rowlands, who visited Mary Jones almost daily in the last 3 years of Mary's life. Lewis died on the 19th July 1887, aged 77 and was buried at Llanycil on the 22nd July 1887. Jane died in June 1892 and was buried at Llanycil on the 6th June aged 78. Their son Thomas Charles Edwards was born on the 22nd September 1837 at Bala and he became the first Principal of the University College of Wales at Aberystwyth. He resigned the post in 1891 partly due to ill

health and partly to follow his father as Head of the Theological College at Bala.

Thomas Charles Edwards married Mary Elizabeth Roberts in the spring of 1867 and the couple had 4 children. Thomas died on the 22nd March 1900, aged 62 at Bala.

The second child was Sarah Charles who was baptised at Llanycil on the 17th February 1787. Three weeks before she was born, her mother was taken seriously ill. Thomas refers to this in a letter written to a Mr Mayor on the 23rd March 1787 when he says:

'What 'vague report' you have heard of dear Mrs C -, I do not know; but the truth is this:- she was taken extremely ill about three weeks before her time: but the Lord in mercy wonderfully interposed. I was obliged to live above a week (and a most trying week it was) tossed between hope and fear. She was extremely reduced and her strength was very nearly exhausted. The whole of her recovery is the Lord's doing, and I believe in answer to prayer in extremity.'

Statue of Lewis Edwards outside the College of Bala

Y PARCH
LEWIS EDWARDS
M·A D·D

Baby Sarah sadly died on the 22nd January 1788 and was buried on the 23rd January 1788 in Llanycil churchyard. On the day of her burial, Thomas wrote the following to Mr Mayor, part of which is reproduced:

'Bala Jan 23 1788
I write this to you from the house of mourning. My little girl died yesterday, after a twelve months existence in this our world, in almost continual affliction and sorrow. At last death prevailed and separated her soul from her afflicted body, to meet again when both the one and the other will be fuller of holiness and felicity than they were here of sin and sorrow. How free was the grace that saved her and took her to glory ! It came to her unthought of, unsought for, and undesired. Her sin was taken away without any sorrow for it, hatred towards it, or striving against it. Without any contest she got the victory for ever over all the enemies of our souls ! Without travelling one step of the wilderness-road she got safe to Canaan. The grace planted within her is got to its full growth without the nurture and discipline which others require and are exercised with. Here it was but as seed under-grown; but now it is full-grown and loaded with the richest fruits. Blessed be God for his full

salvation ! I think myself happy to be the parent of this little vessel of mercy to be filled with eternal glory. 'The Lord gave; the Lord hath taken away' – nothing but his own; 'blessed be the name of the Lord !'

Sarah shares a grave memorial with her brother Thomas Rice Charles and her memorial reads

'To the memory of
Sarah infant daughter of the
Rev Thomas Charles BA.
She died in the year 1788,
aged 1 year.'

David Jones Charles was the couple's third and last child and he was baptised at Llanycil on the 13th October 1793 and he trained to be a Physician and practised in Bala. In 1805, David was taken under the wing of a Private Tutor, Rev Peter Guillebaud MA in Clapham, London. The Reverend and his wife took in 8 children to tutor at a cost of £40 a year each. By 1811 David was back in Bala and in a footnote to a letter his father wrote on the 17th September, he says:

'Our youngest son is with
an Apothecary and Surgeon in
this Town. The calling he
chose himself.'

By the late autumn of 1812, David was coming to the end of his apprenticeship and in a letter dated 20th October 1812; Thomas is asking his friend Joseph Tarn the following:

'My youngest son is out of his
Apprenticeship at Christmas.
He will want to come to London:
if you should hear of any gentleman in the medical line who will want an Assistant, who is also a serious character, I would be much obliged to you for recommending my son. He is a sober, tractable, good tempered young man and fond of his profession. He is not so bright as solid, and to be depended upon.

I am told there is such a character of the name of Brougham, Finsbury Place, that would prove to him a desirable situation and that he is likely at this time to be in want of such a young man. If you should be going that way I shall be much obliged to you, for turning and making the inquiry. I have every satisfaction in my son's moral conduct hitherto, tho' not a spiritual man. A situation in a truly religious family for him would be a great comfort to his mother and myself.'

David died aged just 28 in December 1821 and was buried in Llanycil churchyard on the 24th December 1821. He never married.

Thomas Charles began his education at Llandowror village school and in 1769 he went to Carmarthen Academy until in 1775 he went to Jesus College, Oxford and obtained a BA in 1779. He was ordained into the Church in 1778 and was a Curate at various churches in Somerset until 1783. It was on a visit to North Wales in 1778 with a friend, Simon Lloyd, that Thomas first met Sally Jones, the daughter of a Bala Shopkeeper and who had taken over her father's business on his death.

Exactly when the couple were first introduced is not certain but in a letter to Simon Lloyd dated 22nd November 1779, Thomas makes the following mention:

'I thank my friend for ye favourable Intelligence you have kindly communicated to me concerning dear Miss Jones. I frequently think of her, and should think much more were not my thoughts necessarily employed of late about other important and unexpected affaires; which when they are settled I believe My Dear Sally will engross more of my Time and thoughts.'

Sara Eade

Gravestone of Thomas Rice Charles & family

Bala

Following their first meeting, the courtship was carried on by letter and she must have made a deep impression on him as his first letter to her starts:

'My very dear friend – Such an unexpected address from a Person who never saw you but once, and that at such a long interval of Time, will I suppose at first not a little surprise you; however I flatter myself that thus circumstanced it comes with the more recommendation, when I assure you that long as the interval is since I had the pleasure of seeing you, you have not been absent from my mind, for a whole day, from that time to this. The first report of your character (which I heard at Carmarthen by some of our religious friends about six years ago) left such an impression on my mind as, I am sure, no length of time can obliterate. I immediately conceived an ardent desire, and a secret hope, that my Heavenly Father's wise and good Providence would so order subsequent events that I should in due time see that beloved person of whom I had formed such a favourable opinion. When Mr Lloyd gave me a kind invitation to spend part of the summer with him at Bala, 'tis inexpressible what secret pleasure and joy the prospect of seeing you afforded me – Nor was I disappointed – The sight of so much good sense, beauty and unaffected modesty, joined with that genuine Piety which eminently adorns your person, administered Fuel to the Fire already enkindled, and which has continued burning with increasing ardour from that Time to this. I should then have explained to you what this letter informs you of, had not difficulties (then insurmountable) been in the way, originating from circumstances which I hope at some future period you'll give me leave to acquaint you with.

Ever since I came to England I have anxiously expected (and not without some foundation, as assured by my friends) that some favourable circumstance would open a door for my return to Wales (a place for ever dear!) but hitherto I have been disappointed. Finding that any longer delay would serve only to distract my mind, and by constant uneasiness in some degree, unfit me for the proper discharge of that very important office in which I am engaged. I determined upon the resolution which I now put in execution, of writing to you, and solicit the favour of a correspondence with you till such Time as kind Providence indulges us with an interview, which on my part is most ardently desired. This favour I hope no impediment stands in the way preventing your granting it me all, but that of a previous engagement, I trust can easily be removed – Be perfectly assured that nothing but real regard and sincere affection for your person only, could ever induce me to write or speak to you on such a subject – You are the only person that ever I saw (and the first I ever addressed on the subject), with whom I thought I could spend my life in happy union and felicity, and for whom I possessed that particular affection and esteem requisite for conjugal happiness: and you are the only temporal blessing I have for some time past asked with importunity of the Lord – I hope that your determination will happily convince me that the Lord's answer is favourable – I shall be present with you when you peruse this, how anxious I shall be for your determination; 'tis impossible to tell you how happy would I deem myself, could I be really present then to confirm to your full satisfaction what I assert in this letter! But as that at present is impossible, I hope to commit this, as well as all other events to Him, who rules supremely in the whole Universe, and orders all things in the best manner for the advancement of His own glory, and the Eternal welfare of His people, and no doubt will order this even for our mutual happiness – To whose mercy and protection, I shall not fail to recommend you by constant prayers, and intersessions for you, which are never more ardent and sincere than when you are interested in them.

I shall anxiously wait for a letter from you – I hope it will be favourable – Communicate your thoughts with freedom, and without the least reserve, for you may depend with unshaken confidence, upon the most inviolable secrecy from me, if required, so to anything you shall please to communicate – Should you be so disposed. I have no manner of objection to you showing this or any subsequent letter to Mr Foulkes, in that I beg his acceptance of my Christian Love, and best respects; My dearest friend, Pray for me, and believe me with the most sincere and invariable affection,

Your most unfeigned friend and humble servant

Thomas Charles

December 28th 1779'

The first two letters from Sally to Thomas no longer exist but she was happy to encourage his advances as further letters from Thomas to Sally show and a postscript to a letter written on the 27th January 1780 begins to show just how much he felt for her:.

'My Dearest Love! I shall be most wretchedly miserable till I come and see you –Days will be weeks, weeks Months and Months years till ye happy blessed period arrives. However, tho' it is absolutely impossible at present, for many reasons, yet I hope at ye conclusion of this Year I shall be able to contrive to spend 3 weeks or a Month at Bala – farewell!'

We have to remember that in the 1780s there was no telephone and the only means of communication was by letter delivered by Mail Coaches (horses and carriage). There were specific postal routes set up across the country and the cost of the letter depended on the distance the letter had to travel. The general 1d post only came in, in 1840

The route a letter from Thomas to Sally might well have taken is - Queen Camel – Sherbourne – Yeovil – Salisbury – Bath – Bristol – Gloucester –Worcester – Ludlow – Shrewsbury – Corwen and finally to Bala. Mail Coaches were large heavy vehicles pulled by at least four horses and the horses were changed on a regular basis along the route at Coaching Inns and as well as the mail the coaches could carry up to six people. The driver was armed and accompanied by an armed guard. He carried a sealed clock and a time bill was entered with the exact time of arrival and departure of the coach at each stage. The guard was provided with a long straight horn, at the sound of which, other travellers on the road gave way, toll gates were opened in advance, all at a fantastic speed not seen before. In 1786 the journey from London to Edinburgh, a distance of 400 miles, could be accomplished in something like sixty hours.

The first letter from Sally that is still in existence is dated the 16th March 1780 and is as follows:

'Revd Sir – I hope your disposition is removed, and your life prolonged for future usefulness in the land of the living – It would have affected me more Pleasure to hear you were well, than to have a proof of your sincerity towards an unworthy object – If that Charity which hopeth all things, admits me the place of a Christian friend in your heart, it is more than I have merit to claim, and all the esteem I can desire or wish – I do not know what happiness there may be in conjugal union, whose friendship is grounded on that Christian Love you have described, I think it bids me fair for happiness in the nearest connection; but it would be a bold adventure to prove it – I must look at this at some great distance, or as a thing never to come to pass, or the thought will be intolerable – The wheel of Providence is in a good Hand, and I can be easy about it – If we had it to turn for ourselves we were undone, for we are often blind to our own happiness, and seek it where it is least to be found – Some seek it in Riches, others in honour; but these are perishing things, and always on the wing as Doctor Watts expresses it.

*'Glittering Stones, and golden things
Wealth and honour that have wings
Ever fluttering to be gone
I could never call my own.'*

I can't suppose these to be your aim, there are no golden mines in poor Bala – I also know what it is to despise these trifles in comparison to the beauty of Godliness, or the image of God in a believer – I detest the thought even in the darkest hour of temptation of having for a friend here, one that must be excluded from bliss to all eternity – But from whence cometh this freedom for me to write? I hope it will not be subject to the remarks of any other person besides yourself? Why is it supposed it is the outside of my letters I wish to conceal? Is not this intended to wave my request? And free you from the engagement of keeping them to yourself? I see no danger of my suspicion of our correspondence arising from thence. If I do I'll follow your advice, without there is occasion I would rather not so it for it will rise in my Father a curiosity to see my letters – It is already as great as I can manage – He thinks he has a right to see your letters, there is no hiding them from him – I hope your change of situation is agreeable, and it is ordered for the good of many – I trust it is your greatest comfort in your ministry to be a blessing to Precious souls – It can't be otherwise to one who has tasted that the Lord is gracious – May the Lord plentifully water His Inheritance, and move His clouds as seemeth Him good – I dare not make an application of the last page of yr letter to myself – I know if I had faith but as a grain of mustard seed, it would enable me to do it, for Jesus is a mighty Saviour, able to keep what is given, against that Day. Nothing but unbelief doubts His willingness.

*'Who seeks His face, who knows His Love, who feel on Earth His power to Love,
Shall ask the Monster where is thy Sting? And where is thy Victory, boasting grave.'*

I am, Your well wisher

Sally Jones'

The letters continued and on Monday 4th September 1780 Thomas began the journey to Bala. He recorded this in his diary as:

"Sept 4 – Set out for Bala to visit ye dear object of my most tender affections for ye first Time – in ye morning experienced a Spirit of prayer, yt ye Lord would be with me, comfort me with his presence, support me by his power and direct me with his holy Spirit – preventing me from taking any one Step without consulting him and knowing his will – I was also enabled in some degree to believe he would be with me in this important affair. Lord keep me from following my own will and inclination in it.'

He arrived in Bala on Friday 8th September recorded in his diary thus:

'about 8 o' th' clock in ye evening arrived safe at ye place of our destination after a long fatiguing journey. Had ye happiness of meeting all my friends well which was no small comfort.'

The correspondence and visits continued with both Thomas and Sally along with Thomas' friend Simon Lloyd looking for Curacies nearer to Bala and in a letter from Sally to Thomas dated the 29th May 1781, she is able to tell him of a vacancy for a Curate at Oswestry. Thomas wrote, at once to the Rev Thomas Trefor but his application was not successful.

By the autumn of 1782, Thomas had accepted a curacy at South Barrow in Somerset. His dream of being able to get a position much closer to Bala seemed even further away. By June 1783 Thomas made a leap of faith and left Somerset. He recorded the following in his diary:

Detail from the plaque on the front of Barclays Bank

June 23. I left Milbourn Port this morn – fully persuaded, by ye consequence what it will, it was the will of God I should do so.'

He took his time travelling to Bala staying with friends along the way and eventually arrived in Bala between Monday the 14th July and Wednesday the 16th July 1783. The couple were married on the 20th August and the entry in the Register at Llanycil reads as follows:

'Thomas Charles of this Parish Batchelor and Sarah Jones of this same Parish were married in this Church by License this twentieth day of August in the Year One Thousand seven hundred and eighty three by me John Lloyd Curate In the Presence of Simon Lloyd Lydia Lloyd'

His diary entry for the day included the following:

'This morning I was married – and I hope I can with truth say 'in ye Lord'. I have seen much of ye Lord's goodness both in ye person he had bestowed upon me and in his manner of giving her – ye Person most suitable in every view of all others I ever saw; and in manner in which she has been

given me was best of all calculated to bring me to a right spirit in asking her and in receiving her of my heavenly Father.'

Sally did not want to leave Bala, so Thomas settled in Bala with his new wife and sought various Curacies in the North Wales area – Llangynog in Montgomeryshire, Bryneglwys in Denbighshire and Llan yr Mawddwy in Merionethshire.

Thomas was an evangelical and the churches he was preaching in found his approaches unconventional and did not fit in with the views of the church in general, at that time. On the 2nd July 1784 he was enrolled as a member of the Methodist Society in Bala. Thomas now became a Preacher amongst the Welsh Calvinistic Methodists.

The home of Thomas & Sally Charles, now Barclays Bank

From very early on in his career as a Preacher, Thomas was shocked at the lack of knowledge about the scriptures amongst the people in his congregations. The circulating schools which has been set up by Griffith Jones and Bridget Bevan had come to an end and Thomas was resolved to provide an alternative. He trained people to become teachers, who in small groups, travelled around, staying in a community for a time teaching people to read and the principles of religion. The Teachers were paid £10 a year from collected funds and by the Methodist Societies in North Wales. Thomas soon realised that the schools needed to meet weekly and promoted the idea of these meetings being on Sundays. Many Chapels held these sessions in the afternoon between the morning and evening services.

In 1799 Thomas began a quarterly publication entitled 'Trysorfa Ysprydol' and in 1805 he compiled a Biblical Dictionary; and a Doctrinal Catechism in 1807. These two works were in use throughout the 19th century. In 1813 he published 'Rules' for the conduct of Sunday Schools. However what was needed most was a constant supply of Welsh Bibles.

The Society for Promoting Christian Knowledge (SPCK) had helped with the printing of Welsh Bibles but not in large enough quantities to fill the need being created by the Sunday School Teachers. Thomas was a member of the Religious Tract Society and at a meeting of the Society in 1802, he put forward an appeal for more Bibles in the Welsh language.

On the 7th March 1804 the British and Foreign Bible Society was formed (now called The Bible Society) by a group of Christians which included William Wilberforce (1759 – 1833, an English Politician and Philanthropist and a leader of the movement to abolish the slave trade) and Thomas Charles; with the clear aim of encouraging the wider circulation and use of the scriptures.

Thomas Charles died on the 5th October 1814 aged just 58 at his home in Bala and he was buried on the 7th October 1814 in Llanycil churchyard. Sally lived on for only a short while and she died on the 24th October 1814 aged 61. She was buried with her husband on the 28th October 1814.

A few weeks after their death the following letter was written by Mrs Foulkes of Machynlleth to a Mrs Lees of the Priory, Shrewsbury:

Thomas Charles in later life
(from an engraving executed in 1839)

Sara Eade Collection

Sara Eade

Capel Tegid, Bala

the world of mary jones

31

'Dear Cousin – I have been thinking of writing to you for many weeks passed, but either lowness of Spirits, ill-health, or hurry of business have prevented me hitherto.

You know we have been again visited with another severe affliction in the loss of our beloved and most valued friends of Bala, the Revd Thos Charles, and Mrs Charles, his wife, for whom we mourn and much regret.

The changes in that family were awful and sudden! My daughter, Sarah, went to Bala to see our afflicted friends after they had buried their old and trusty and pious Servant Peggy; who had lived with them nine years, and was greatly valued by them.

Mr Charles said that the storm had been very black, and the clouds gloomy, by losing Peggy, by his son having been in a dangerous way, and by his being himself very ill. But

He hoped the clouds were beginning to wear a little brighter; He was at that time a little better, and walked in Sarah's arm about the room: His conversation with her was very heavenly and much upon another world; He quoted many passages of Scripture, namely, 'For this corruptible must put on incorruption; and this mortal must put on immorality; It is sown in dishonour, it is raised in glory etc. There remaineth a rest for the people of God. A better country they sought, and that was a heavenly one.' He exhorted her to seek those better things; as they were the things that would make her happy here, and fitter for that better company.

On the Monday, before he took his final adieu! Of all below, He wished Mrs Charles and Mary would take an airing in his Gig, and that Sarah would accompany them upon his Mare; as Mary had been much confined. They did as He wished; and, during that time, He went to see his Son, who was then confined, and stopped with him half an hour; and the pious Father's conversation, in this his last interview with his eldest Son, was, doubtless, weighty and heavenly. Tuesday morning Sarah wrote a few lines to me by a person who was coming hither that night, saying, she hoped Mr Charles was in a way of recovering, but very weak. But Oh! How sudden the change came on! On Wednesday morning about six o'clock He happened to alter for the worse, and at ten o'clock in the morning he finished his labors and sorrows! A special Messenger was on that Day despatched to Carmarthen to inform his eldest and pious Brother of this awful event; who brought us the melancholy tidings. It is easier to conceive that to describe our feelings upon this sorrowful event!

Mr D Charles, and Miss Charles came hither on Friday night. I accompanied them in a chaise to Bala; which place we reached at 8 o'clock on Saturday morning;-and, to our great disappointment found Mr Charles had been buried the day before – which affected his Brother and myself more than I can express.

Mr Charles's corpse was buried so soon by the persuasion of the Doctor; altho' it was evident; there was no necessity for such a hurry. We can only exclaim with the inspired writer, 'A great man is fallen in Israel.'

His end was, like the setting sun, becoming brighter and brighter as it descended towards the Horizon, until it disappeared in Glory. Poor Mrs Charles's health was much impaired in consequence of losing her dear Mr Charles. Sometimes her recollection failed her so much, that she had no idea of his death. When she was convinced how things were, she would weep and wonder how he was taken before her.

It was in much love and tender mercy that her sorrows were put to an end too, so suddenly after his removal; he dying on October 5th and she on October 24th 1814.

The day before she died, she and her youngest Son, Dr David Charles, were in the Tea Room, the family were gone to Chapel. She said, Let us go a little to prayer; her Ideas were collected, clear, and spiritual, both for herself and for her son, - the following night she was put in bed as usual about seven o'clock. The maid stopt in the room till she slept, and had been upstairs several times, and finding her in a comfortable and sound sleep, gave Mary a hint, least she should disturb her, by going to bed, as they both slept together. As Mary was raising the clothes to go to bed, she perceived that Mrs Charles looked paler than usual, and cried out, 'Oh! I am afraid she is dead!' It was a sudden shock to her feelings; as it was to the family.

Mary came home last Friday, in company with Mr David (Jones) Charles; who is to return to London in a few weeks.

Miss Charles of Carmarthen is to make some stay in Bala, and before her return home, is to stop with us for some time. And it is proposed for Sarah to accompany her to Carmarthen on a visit.

My daughters unite with me in kind love to Mr Lees and family &c, &c, &c.

I remain Dear Cousin, Yours truly affectionate

Lydia Foulkes Nov 1814'

The base of the Thomas Charles' Monument

Thomas Charles' is standing on 3 Bibles

One side of the base of the Thomas Charles'

Thomas Charles left a Will which made provision for his family as follows:

'I Thomas Charles of the town of Bala in the County of Merioneth Clerk being of sound and disposing mind memory and understanding do make my last will and testament as follows That is to say My immortal soul I commit to Him who gave it and died to redeem me a guilty and helpless sinner. In this last surrender of myself I have full satisfaction and confidence of my being graciously accepted in the beloved Son of God who is all my salvation and all my desire. As to the interment of my mortal part I leave that wholly to the discretion of my Executrix hereinafter mentioned. Whereas I am the owner of the Inheritance of three messuages or dwelling houses with their appurtenances two of them situate in Bala aforesaid and the other in Hope Street in the town of Manchester in the County of Lancaster now I do hereby give all the same premises unto my dear wife Sarah Charles for her natural life. And from and immediately after her death I give all that my house situate in Bala aforesaid with its appurtenances now in the occupation of my eldest son Thomas Rice Charles being one of my said three houses unto my said eldest son for his natural life and in case of the determination of his life estate therein by forfeiture or otherwise in his lifetime I give my said house left to him as aforesaid with its appurtenances from and immediately after such determination of his life estate therein unto my brother David Charles and his heirs during the natural life of my said son in trust to support the contingent estate hereinafter limited thereof and for that purpose to make entries and bring actions as occasion may require but yet to permit my said son to take the rents and profits thereof to his own use during his natural life. And from and after the death of my said son I give my said house with its appurtenances hereinbefore left to him unto all and every his child or children who shall be living at his death or born in due time after and all and every the child or children of any child or children of his who may have died in his lifetime and to their heirs as tenants in common but the issue of every such deceased child of his shall take only such part or share thereof as every such deceased child would have taken if he or she had been living at the death of my said son And as to any other house in Bala aforesaid which is now in my occupation and my said house in Manchester I give the same with their appurtenances from and after the death of my said wife unto my youngest son David Charles for his natural life And from and after the determination of his life estate therein if it shall happen by any means in his lifetime I give the same two houses with their appurtenances unto my said brother and his heirs during the natural life of my said youngest son in trust merely to support the contingent estates hereinbefore limited

Thomas Charles' monument outside Capel Tegid, Bala

thereof by all proper acts in law but yet to suffer my said youngest son to take the rents and profits thereof to his own use during his natural life and from and after the death of my said youngest son I give my said two houses with their appurtenances hereinbefore left to him to all and every his child and children who shall be living at his death or born after and the issue if any of every deceased child of his shall have died in his lifetime and to their heirs for ever as tenants in common but the issue of every deceased child of his shall have only such share as every such deceased child would have taken if he or she had been living at the death of my said youngest son. And if my said youngest son shall happen to depart his life without leaving any issue in whom upon his death my said two houses hereinbefore left to him shall vest under the preceding clause of this my will in that case from and immediately after his death I give my said last mentioned two houses with their appurtenances to my said eldest son for his natural life with remainder as I have before limited my said other house to my said brother and his heirs during the life of my said eldest son to support contingent remainder or remainders to all and every the child and children of my said eldest son living at his death or born in due time after and the issue of any deceased child or children of his and their heirs for ever as tenant in common the issue of every deceased child taking only such share as the parent of such issue if living at the death of my said eldest son would have taken. And whereas the several sums of two thousand and five hundred pounds are now owing to me from my said eldest son on two several bonds from him to me. Now I do hereby give the interest of those two sums to my dear wife Sarah for her life and after her death

I give the interest thereof to my said eldest son for his life and after his death I give the said two sums to all and every his child and children living at his death or born in due time after and the issue of every child of his who may have died in his lifetime equally among them except that the issue of every deceased child shall take only what the parent if living at my said eldest son's death would have taken And Whereas I have laid out two thousand five hundred pounds in the purchase of stock in the four per cents which now belongs to me Now I do hereby give the dividend of that my stock property and of any other money that I may have in the funds at my death unto my said wife for her life and after her death I give the dividends of my said stock in the four per cents purchased as aforesaid with the sum of two thousand five hundred pounds to my said youngest son for his life and after his death I give my said last mentioned stock property unto all and every his child and children living at his death or born in due time after and the issue of every child of his who may have died in his lifetime equally among them except that the issue of every deceased child of his shall take only what a parent would have taken if living at the death of my said youngest son and if my said youngest son shall die without issue living at his death or born in due time after and without issue of any child of his that shall have died in his lifetime I then give the dividend of the said stock purchased as aforesaid with the sum of two thousand five hundred unto my said eldest son for his life and after death I give the said mentioned stock to the child and children of my eldest son and the issue of any deceased child of his I have before given to them the said several sums of two thousand pounds and five hundred

pounds I give after the death of my said wife the interest of one hundred pounds to my niece Mrs Rebecca Saunderson for her life and after her death I give such sum of one hundred pounds to her child or children living at her death and the issue of any of her children who may have died in her lifetime equally among them except that the issue of every deceased child shall take no more than what the parent would have taken if living at the death of my said niece. The residue of my personal estate I give to my said wife for ever except that after her death my household goods and furniture plate linen and china shall belong to my said youngest son. In case my executors shall think it expedient I wish them to call in the said money due on the bonds of my eldest son and to place it out on other good security and I do hereby appoint my said wife and Griffith Richards of Glanllyn near Bala aforesaid Gentleman and my said brother the executrix and executors of this my will and in testimony of this being my will I have to the three first sheets thereof set my name and to the last sheet thereof my name and seal the twentieth day of December in the year of our Lord one thousand eight hundred and thirteen.

Thomas Charles

Signed sealed published and declared in the presence of us who have in the testators' presence and of each other signed our names as witnesses ...... John Reynolds Queen Street, Chester John Walker, Brazier, Chester David Fra. Jones, Chester

A carved slate plate was attached to Charles' tomb which reads as follows:

'Underneath lie the remains of
The Revd Thomas Charles BA of Bala
Who died Oct 5, 1814 aged 59.
By his indefatigable endeavours when in London (AD 1804) to
Procure a supply of the Holy Scriptures for the use of his
Native countrymen he became the means of establishing
The BRITISH and FOREIGN BIBLE SOCIETY.
He was the Reviver of the Welsh Circulating Charity Schools
and a most active Promoter of Sunday Schools both for Children
and Adults:- and North Wales (the more immediate field of his
ministerial labours for 30 years) will probably retain traces of
his various and strenuous exertions to promote the kingdom
of Christ till time shall be no more.
Also SARAH, Relict of the above THOMAS CHARLES
Died Oct 24th 1814 aged 61.
She was possessed of every natural endowment and
Divine grace and was an helpmeet indeed to the
Man, the Christian and the Minister.

Sara Eade

Memorial plaque on the end of Thomas Charles' grave at Llanycil.

Rev David Erwyd Jenkins wrote three volumes of 'The Life of Thomas Charles' and he had access to a great deal of letters, diaries and other material relating to Thomas Charles and his family. The Rev Jenkins did not find any references in either Thomas's diaries or in any letters relating specifically to Mary Jones or a girl who had walked a great distance to Bala to obtain a Welsh Bible. However there are lots of references to the lack of knowledge of the scriptures amongst church attenders and Thomas himself was very much aware as to how few Welsh Bibles were available.

Library at the College in Bala

Llanycil Church

Lewis Edwards

Thomas Charles' Grave

Bala Bridge

A room in Bala College

Bala Lake

Bala College

The Farm opposite Tyn y Ddol

Welsh Long House - Has extra room, was used to house animals in the winter

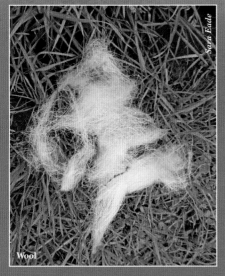

Wool

In the late 1700s the sea came inland as far as Bird Rock, which is now one of the furthest places inland where cormorants come to roost. The land was later drained as part of an agricultural experiment carried out by Edward Corbet. Edward wanted fertile land in a sheltered environment to grow vegetables and fruit. The Corbet family owned much of the area, having built up their holdings following their settlement in the area at Ynysmaengwyn, their summer residence, from their base at Moreton Corbet in Shropshire.

The keeping of sheep was the main part of Hill Farming and many of the industries in the area were linked to the by-product of sheep – wool. Sheep were the only animals who could survive the harsh environment, though most farmers did have chickens, pigs and a house cow. Cow's milk was made into butter and cheese and was only drunk when someone was ill. Most of the farmers would take their excess butter and cheese to a local shop where it was sold. There was often some competition involved as some people were better at making butter and cheese than others and demand for butter or cheese from a specific farm was keenly sought. Each farm had its own mark which was pressed into the butter and this made it easier for customers to buy the butter they liked best.

Sara Eade

Bake Oven

Bees were kept for their honey and most people had a vegetable patch where much needed vegetables, herbs and fruit, such as apples, blackberries and strawberries were grown. Other sources of food included rabbits and game as well as fish from the river and the sea. The surrounding countryside also provided such things as hazelnuts and rosehips from which syrup was made.

Cottages, known as Welsh Longhouses were built from local stone and often of one storey with a low pitched slate or turfed roof with two small windows in the front wall. A front door opened straight in the main living area which was dominated by the fireplace, where a fire was always kept burning. This was the only source of heat, the only source of hot water and the only means of cooking. Close by the fire was stored the peat and wood used to fuel the fire, the residual heat from the fire allowed the wood and peat to dry.

Life was hard, all the cooking was from basic ingredients and cooked on the open fire (though some cottages did have a bake oven), washing was done by hand and the nearest shop was more than two miles away at Abergynolwyn and the local people relied very much on what they could produce at home. The nearest market towns were at Towyn and Dolgellau and it was a common sight to see animals being herded to market along the traditional Drovers' Roads.

The bake oven was a wall oven set into the fireplace. This was usually brick lined with an arch shaped roof and a flat bottom. A fire, using wood was set on the flat bottom. The temperature was judged by the change in colour of the bricks. When the correct temperature was reached the fire was taken out and whatever was being cooked was placed in the oven.

Items requiring a high temperature were cooked first and as the oven cooled down other items requiring a lower temperature were cooked. Often the last thing that went in was a rice pudding as this would cook in a lower temperature and would stay warm until required at the evening meal. After food had been cooked, damp or wet wood would be placed in the oven to dry out and be ready for the next time the oven was needed.

Lighting was natural during the day and oil lamps and candles were used sparingly at night. For those who could not afford candles, reeds were collected during the summer, dried out and then soaked in fat. These could be lit for light but soon burnt through.

The day was governed by daylight so the working day was longer in summer than in winter. Whilst adults slept in the main living area, children often slept in the loft, which was accessed by a ladder. A mattress of hay, straw or feathers covered with hand woven blankets kept the cold out in winter. Feathers from the farmyard fowl were also used for pillows.

The village itself was a series of Hill Farms and a couple of small clusters of cottages – one around Tyn y Ddol and one around the church. One of the houses opposite the church was the village pub.

Sara Eade

This house, opposite the Church, used to be the village pub

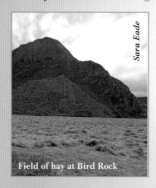

Sara Eade

Field of hay at Bird Rock

Sara Eade

Though not in Mary's time the village still has a postbox

Cwrt is one of the two hamlets that now make up Abergynolwyn and is situated alongside the Afon Dysynni, which drains the Talyllyn Lake down to The Broad Water and the sea. At Cwrt the Afon Dysynni is joined by the Gwernol and provides the hamlet with water on three sides. This was very advantageous in years gone by when machinery was powered by water.

Some of the cottages at Cwrt date back to around 1700 and, at one time, it was the site of the village tannery, an industry which, required large quantities of water. The first Methodist Chapel, in the area, was built at Cwrt and was the one that Mary and her mother attended. It was built in 1806 and in a Religious Survey taken in 1851 the following was said of it:

'Cwrt Chapel Calvinistic Methodist Erected 1806 Not used exclusively as a place of worship Not a separate building Attendance Morning 41 scholars Afternoon 104 Evening 63'

The information was given by John Vaughan, Elder, of Maesllan near Dolgelley.

Today the chapel has been converted into two holiday homes and is just one of four redundant chapels in Abergynolwyn and Cwrt.

The industries operating in Cwrt provided much of the employment for the village. Many local people worked at the tannery. The women harvested the oak bark, an essential ingredient providing the tannin needed to cure the hides, which was the job of the men. The tanning liquid was made by adding dried oak bark to cold water and allowing the mixture to stand for several weeks before use. Although it was only a small tannery, it provided all the leather for local needs. Oak bark was also exported by ships, from Barmouth to Ireland for which the Irish paid £13 13s a ton.

Many local farmers included the growing of oak trees and the harvesting of the bark as an essential part of the farming year. Felled timber was selling for 3s a foot at this time.

There was even a brewery at Cwrt!

The other main industry at Cwrt was the production of wool. A fulling mill was located in Cwrt and was in existence as early as 1808. There were also Fulling Mills at Maes y Pandy (a farm close to the church at Talyllyn Lake) and Dolammerch by Pentre (rear of the village hall and at the bottom of what was later to become the village incline, in Abergynolwyn and which allowed the slate wagons to be brought down into the village as well as coal and other goods which had come up from Tywyn by rail).

Webs, lengths of woven cloth, were put into a mixture of stale urine; pigs dung and fullers earth (soapy clay). This process removed the lanolin and the grease from the wool and shrank the thread. Once the webs had been soaked and beaten at the mill, they were taken to the tentering rack. Webs were approximately 7/8ths of a yard wide and 120-180 feet long and were woven on looms by outworkers who worked in their own homes. The hammers used in the fulling process were made of wood and were ungoverned - the faster the stream flowed, the faster the hammers beat the webs. Having machinery powered by water and ungoverned could be very dangerous as there was no way of slowing the machine down other than by stopping the water which powered it.

There was also a small woollen mill at Cwrt until around 1900. It was located in one of the houses alongside the bridge and the machinery was driven by water-power.

There were two shops in Cwrt, one just by the edge of the village and now known as 'Hen Siop'. For some years it has been a bed and breakfast but today is a private house. The other was on the other edge of the village and known as Upper Shop, though now called Glanafon. This shop was a tailor's and there was also a milliner based there as well. Gentlemen could purchase suits here as well as working trousers and waistcoats whilst the ladies could have a new hat.

The censuses help us to understand how the hamlet developed. On the 1841 census only 9 cottages are listed and the main trade of those living in the cottages was Farmers or Farm Servants.

By 1871 there are 12 cottages listed and two shops. At one of the shops is John Williams aged 34, a Grocer and Draper with his wife Margaret aged 32 and children, David aged 8, Evan O aged 7, John J aged 3 and Margaret W aged 2. At the other shop was David Jones aged 32 a Grocer and Joiner. The occupations of the workers living in the cottages, was mostly Slate Quarrier or Quarryman (Slate).

On the 1881 census living at 'Shop Uchaf' is Thomas Edwards aged 38, a Tailor and Draper together with his wife Eliza aged 31 and three children, Eliza J aged 7, Mary M aged 5 and Willie O aged 4. There are 13 cottages listed with the occupations mostly being Slate Miners, At 'Shop Cwrt' was David Rowlands but he was a Slate Quarryman. Living with him and his family was Mary Davies, a lodger who was aged 26 and carrying on the business of a Milliner and Dressmaker.

By 1891, 'Shop Ucha' is a William Edwards aged 52, a Tailor and Draper and his wife Catherine aged 51. Living with them were two lodgers and Sally Edward, niece aged 15. Thirteen cottages are listed and we now see some different occupations for along with Slate Quarrymen are Boot Seller and General Hawker, Tailor's Apprentice, Washer Woman, Farm Labourer and Game and River Keeper.

On the 1901 census, 15 cottages are listed with occupations such as Quarryman, Washerwoman, Dress Maker, General Labourer, Domestic Servant and Midwife. At Cwrt Shop, John Miles Edwards, aged 46, is a Slate Quarryman but his wife, Mary aged 39, is listed as a Grocer. Living with them are their three children, Hugh Miles aged 10, Sarah Margaret aged 9 and Fanny aged 5.

By 1911 William and Catherine Edwards are at 'Shop Uchaf' and plying the trade of a Tailor. Only six of the cottages are being lived in but only one person has an occupation. Robert Roberts was living at 2 Cwrt and he was a Roadman.

The Railway Inn, once The Red Lion, Abergynolwyn

Abergynolwyn is made of the two small hamlets of Cwrt and Pandy, the latter being a small group of cottages and a pub called The Red Lion (now called The Railway Inn). These two hamlets grew up close to streams which provided water for both everyday life and for industry.

A small village is usually called a hamlet when it doesn't have a church. Until St David's Church, Abergynolwyn, was built, on the outskirts of the village in 1879; the nearest church for worshippers was at St Mary's, Talyllyn, which was shared with the people of Corris until Holy Trinity Church, in Corris was built in 1861.

St. David's Church, Abergynolwyn

St David's Abergynolwyn was built following the expansion of the village in the mid-1860s as a result of the slate quarry at Bryneglwys being developed by the McConnel family who had purchased the leases in the early 1860s. The houses in Tanybryn Street, Water Street and Llanegryn Street were built to provide housing for the slate quarry workers. At the same time, the Talyllyn Railway was built and it started carrying slate down to Towyn in 1865 and passengers in 1866.

In addition to St David's Church there were also four chapels, one in Cwrt, two in Llanegryn Street and one on the main road from Towyn to the Talyllyn Lake.

The oldest house in Abergynolwyn was Tyn y Llion (in English it means land of the mine) and dated back to 1590. It was located close to the bridge and opposite what was later the Police Station. Sadly it was demolished and replaced by a modern house.

From 1810 – 1814 land was being enclosed in this part of Wales. Dry stone walls were being built using stone that was lying on the ground. Many men got jobs building the walls and were paid the

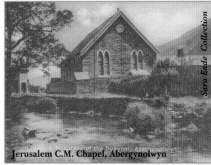

Jerusalem C.M. Chapel, Abergynolwyn

princely sum of 10s (50p) a rood (¼ acre) which worked out to about 6d (3p) a day. In and around Abergynolwyn some land was enclosed using slate posts, linked together with strong wire and these fences can be dated to around 1840 and later as the slate which was used was wastage from the slate being split into roofing slates.

By 1794, the first Day School had been set up, by The Rev Thomas Charles, in Abergynolwyn and it was here that Mary learnt to read and write with John Ellis, a teacher from Barmouth. The current school, which was built in 1883, was closed in 2012 and the children attend an area school at Llanegryn.

Abergynolwyn from above, Cwrt, all 4 chapels are visable. The C.M. Chapel which was in Cwrt is the building in the foreground with 2 chimneys on the roof.

Village of Abergynolwyn from the top of the village incline. Cwrt is the group of houses at the far end of the village.

There was a Post Office in the village, which in later years was in Llanegryn Street in a building that had once been the village smithy and is now a private house.

On the 13th August 1870, new postal arrangements were announced which allowed the Talyllyn Railway to carry the mail up to Abergynolwyn from Towyn. The Cambrian News and Merionethshire Standard carried the announcement:

'TOWYN
New Postal Arrangements – The Postmaster General has made arrangements for the conveyance of letters for Talyllyn, Abergynolwyn, Bryneglwys Quarries &c, via Towyn and thence per Talyllyn Railway, instead of foot post from Machynlleth, as heretofore. Mr Ebenezer Jones has been appointed Postmaster at Abergynolwyn, and a foot postman will carry the letters to and from Talyllyn. The box will close at 3.45 pm. This alteration will much increase the work of Mr Jones, postmaster at Towyn.'

In the Cambrian News and Merionethshire Standard for the 20th August 1870, the following was reported:

'POSTAL DELIVERIES – Post

letters hitherto have been brought to this important slate district on foot via Corris and Talyllyn, and did not reach the village until early in the afternoon, and no time was allowed for replying. Last week through the exertions of our County Member, Mr Holland, a most important improvement took place in the appointment of Mr Ebenezer Jones as postmaster, and in the mails being conveyed from Towyn, per the little railway. Letters now arrive shortly after nine in the morning and are not despatched till 3.30 in the afternoon. Mr McConnell, the chief proprietor of the railway, is also entitled to the thanks of the public for the prompt and liberal way in which he met the wishes of the postal authorities.'

Abergynolwyn looking to Talyllyn

The Postman who collected the mail from Abergynolwyn Station was William Rowlands. William lived with his parents, John and Ann Rowlands in Pandy Square. The Postman's job was not a full-time one and so William also ran a cycle repair business as well.

Above Abergynolwyn is the Gwernol Valley which from about 1840 was the site of slate quarrying which later became known as the Bryneglwys Slate Quarry. In Mary's day this valley was the location of

Abergynolwyn

at least seven dwellings. These were mostly farms or small cottages used by shepherds during the summer months.

The farmhouses of Nant Llwyn-gwedd and Hendrewallog are thought to date from the sixteenth century and both were

built with the long axis down the slope instead of across it, which was a common practice with Welsh Longhouses in this area and were called Medieval Platform Houses. This arrangement allowed the space beneath the floor at the lower end to be used by animals.

Where Welsh Longhouses were built with the axis built across the slope, they often had an extra, covered space built onto the end of the house where the chimney was located. This room was used to house animals in the winter and the residual heat from the chimney helped to keep the space dry. Such a house was Tyn-y-Ddol at Llanfihangel y Pennant where Mary Jones was brought up as a small child.

Bryneglwys farmhouse, also known as Hen-dy (Old House) was a double fronted stone building with a stable built onto the south gable end. Bryneglwys was a large farm and located close to the farmhouse was a barn, a cow shed and a row of very primitive cottages for use by farm hands.

One of these farmhouses had a spiral staircase going up to the upper floor around the inglenook. A similar building is Dolgoed in the Ratgoed valley above Aberllefenni. In this case the staircase went up to a single room where the woollen fleeces were put to dry out using heat that radiated from the chimney and the fire below.

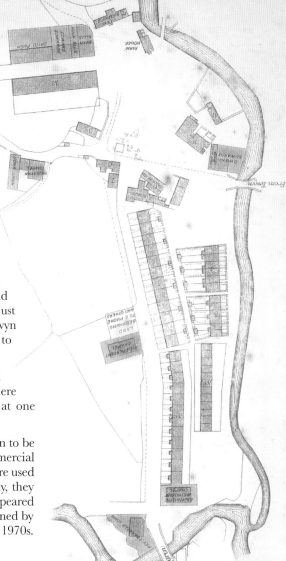

There was also a small holding called Frondeg which was lived in in 1842 by a man named Hen Idris when he was a boy. Frondeg was possibly the oldest of the Medieval Houses and was a Medieval Hall House.

Hendre was a Lateral Chimney House (it had a chimney in the middle of one of the longest outside walls) and it had a summer house located just below the church at Abergynolwyn and adjacent to the road to Towyn.

The farm of Hendrewallog had sheep up at Nant y Nord, where there had also been a house at one time.

When the slate quarrying began to be undertaken on a more commercial basis, many of the buildings were used by slate miners but sadly, today, they are all in ruins. Some have disappeared under slate waste or were flattened by the Forestry Commission in the 1970s.

The village of Abergynolwyn with thge Gwernol valley in the distance

Sara Eade Collection

The Town of Bala

ala was founded in about 1310 by Roger de Mortimer of Chirk Castle, the Justiciar of North Wales. In Medieval times the Justiciar was the equivalent of our modern Prime Minister. Bala was created a free borough, by a Charter in 1324 in the reign of Edward 11 (1307-1327)

Until the passing of the Local Government Act in 1894, Bala was part of the Parish of Llanycil and under the Act, Bala became a separate parish and consequently its own church was built. The church at Llanycil is just over a mile from the town. As early as 1758 petitions were being made to have a church in the town. There had been a Chapel of Ease but it was now in ruins and the distance to Llanycil meant that people had started to meet in houses in the town rather than walk to Llanycil. At that time the estimate for the building of a new church was £1,084.

The name Bala means *'a place where a lake discharges itself into a river'*. It was never a large place and even by 1944 the population was only 1,460. In 2001 the population had only risen to 1,980.

Bala was noted for its fairs and markets, the right to hold them having been granted on the town by its Charter. Prior to 1310 they had been held in the Parish of Llanfor.

Bala was also known for the manufacture of woollen articles such as stockings and gloves and it was not unusual to see women knitting as they walked. Finished items were sold in the market.

One of the earliest buildings in Bala, is the Tower of Bala or the 'Tomen', a tumulus or moat hill thought to be the former site of a Roman Camp. Bala Grammar School was founded in 1712.

In 1837, Lewis Edwards and David Charles opened a preparatory school in Bala and in 1839 this building became a ministerial college for the Calvinistic Methodist Church, which later became the Presbyterian Church. The college is now the national centre for children's and youth work for the Presbyterian Church.

High Street, Bala and White Lion Royal Hotel

High Street, Bala

Llanycil Church

The College, Bala

The village of Bryncrug is two miles from Tywyn on the road to Dolgellau. Its name, in English, means 'Barrow Hill' though some local people believe that the name comes from the hills around the village being covered in heather.

The village has always been small and close knit and centred around agriculture with the village developing alongside the river Fathew and the bridge which crosses it in the centre of the village. In addition to the road, the village is also connected to Tywyn by the Talyllyn Railway and a station at Rhydyronen, about one mile from the village.

Today the village's only shop has been run by the same family for a great number of years and provides a wide range of staple items for both the villagers and visitors alike.

The only public house in the village today is called 'The Peniarth Arms', but was once called the 'The Cross Pipes', and there was a period in the village's history when there was no Public House at all.

There have been several schools in the village over the years but in 2013, the local school closed and the pupils were moved to a new community school at Llanegryn called 'Ysgol Craig Aderyn' (Bird Rock School). Funding is currently being sought to turn the old school building into a community building, thus providing the village with a meeting place.

Sara Eade

St Matthew's Church, Bryncrug

St Matthew's Church was built in 1877 and served the village until 2007 when it was closed and sold. It is now being developed into a private house. The sacramental vessels for St Matthew's church were given by Lady Harlech in 1882 and consisted of the following:

1 A FLAGON which was 9inches tall and made of glass and mounted in silver gilt and the base was set with six jewels.

2 A CHALICE which was made of silver gilt and held three-quarters of a pint of wine. It was 8 inches tall and there were twelve jewels set in the base.

3 A Patern which was 6 inches in diameter and was used to hold the wafers for Communion.

There were at least three chapels in Bryncrug but now only one remains. The Bethlehem Chapel was once a Calvinistic Methodist Chapel and is now a Presbyterian Chapel. The current building replaced the original Chapel building which would have been the one that Mary Jones and her family attended. In the religious survey of 1851, the Bethlehem Chapel had been built in 1800 and in 1851 the attendance was 210 people in the morning, 212 scholars in the afternoon and 250 people attending the evening service. The Steward, at that time, was Griffith Jones of Gwyddelfynedd Farm at Bryncrug (It was here too that Lizzie Jones, later Rowlands, was the Governess)

The Village Pump, Bryncrug

Sara Eade

Brynhoreb Chapel was a Wesleyan Chapel and in the religious survey of 1851, its attendance was 71 in the morning, 67 scholars in the afternoon and 107 in the evening. The Steward was John James who lived at Bryncrug Board School.

In the main, Bryncrug was a quiet village but in August 1892 the following was carried in the '*Cambrian News*':

'HOME RULE AT BRYNCRUG

The heavy death rate of Merionethshire is partly explained by the unintelligent action of the inhabitants of Bryncrug, a village about two miles from Towyn. The inhabitants of Bryncrug obtain their water for drinking purposes from a stream which runs through the place. This stream receives the washings of a woollen factory, runs through three or four farmyards, and passes alongside a crowded graveyard before it reaches Bryncrug, whose inhabitants, with grand disregard for consequences, consume its dirty waters. The death-rate of Bryncrug is heavy. The people are satisfied with the water from the stream, but they think people should be asked not to pollute it. They do not object to the washings from the wool factory, or the liquid manure from the farm years, or the drainage from the burial-place, but they think people should be asked not to pollute the stream which in rainy weather is so muddy that even the hardy inhabitants of Bryncrug cannot drink it until it has settled somewhat! One of the members of the Towyn and Aberdovey Local Board said at the last meeting that now Home Rule was the order of the day the inhabitants of Bryncrug thought the people of Towyn and Aberdovey should not foist

One of the Non Conformist Chapels in Bryncrug, now a private residence

Sara Eade

upon them what they did not require. This is a free country, and if the inhabitants of a village wish to drink wool washings, farm-yard liquid, and grave drippings why should they be interfered with? We are, however, glad to know that there are some discontented inhabitants of Bryncrug who complain to the Sanitary Inspector every time he goes to Bryncrug, that they cannot get a drop of clean water to drink after heavy rain or in a dry summer, to say nothing of people throwing refuse into the stream. Refuse means the contents of bedchamber utensils, dead cats, kitchen refused, and filth of every kind. We put this matter quite plainly, as it well that the people of Bryncrug and of other dirty little places should drink their filth with their eyes open. A meeting of the inhabitants of Bryncrug is to be convened in order that the inhabitants may decide 7whether or not they prefer to go on poisoning themselves. We never like to speculate on the unknown, but we have little doubt that the inhabitants of Bryncrug will decide that the water they use is quite good enough for them, especially if they could be sure that it contained nothing worse than wool washings, liquid manure from farm yards, and drainage from a thickly-peopled graveyard.

It speaks ill for village life in Wales that the inhabitants of places like Bryncrug should ask

in the name of Home Rule to be allowed to use water which is impregnated with all sorts of filth. We have no ill-will against Bryncrug or the other places in Merionethshire where the people drink dirty water. It is in our opinion a plain duty we owe to the people to bring home to them full knowledge of the causes which slay them. Great services are not within our power, but it is within our power to tell the people of Bryncrug that the water they drink is deadly poison. The members of the Towyn and Aberdovey Board talked about the dirty water of Bryncrug quite unconcernedly! The Sanitary Inspector hears complaints, but the people claim the right under Home Rule to drink polluted water and to spread disease and death far and wide. We appeal to ministers, school-masters, members of public bodies, and whoever has influence to make clear to the inhabitants of places like Bryncrug that they destroy their comfort, their health, and their life itself by consuming pollutes water. There is one other point. The Local Board has a duty to perform, and that duty ought to be performed at the risk if needs be of unpopularity. It may be true that the general feeling of the people of Bryncrug who would like to have clean water to drink and they, as well as the less particular sort, have a right to be considered.'

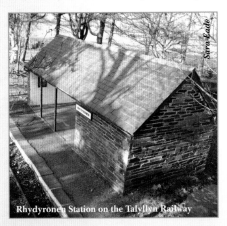

Rhydyronen Station on the Talyllyn Railway

Sara Eade

Sara Eade Collection

Castell y Bere

The Borough of Bere is one of the oldest in Merionethshire and was granted a Charter by Edward I (1272 – 1307) in 1285 but was only nominally a Borough because it contained a castle. The Borough was an undefined area surrounding the castle and containing the farms located close to the castle.

The castle, known as Castell y Bere is situated on a hill in the centre of the Dysynni Valley. Though it doesn't look it today, this position was once one of strategic importance. In years gone by the sea came inland as far as Bird Rock, about a mile or so away from the Castle. In the late 1700s and early 1800s there were two major drainage projects undertaken by the landowners lower down the valley – the Corbets who were originally from Moreton Corbet in Shropshire and had made their summer residence at Ynysmaengwyn (the island of the white rock) at Tywyn. The Corbet family owned the land from the Peniarth estate to the sea and along the coast towards Aberdovey.

The hill commanded a view down to the sea and would easily have prevented troops coming inland as well as preventing troops from inland getting to the sea to escape.

The castle was built in the reign of Henry III (1216 – 1272) and it was on the site of an older castle built by Llywelyn the Great (1194 – 1240), so an English King unwittingly paid a compliment to the military instinct of a Welsh Prince.

The original design is similar to that of a traditional Motte and Bailey design and its construction was probably influenced by earlier Norman castles and the shape of the rock on which it stands.

A leaflet produced in the 1970s by C Graham Benham, details some historical background:

'The Romans, Angles and Saxons were unable completely to subdue the Welsh. The Normans in their conquest of Britain built castles along the Welsh border, called the Marches, and left the Barons to keep the Welsh in check.

Owen Gwynedd did much to unite Wales and on his death left an example of what could be achieved by the talents of military skills and diplomacy. He left seven sons, one of them, Iorwerth, was the father of Llywelyn Fawr (Great) known also as Llywelyn-ap-Iorwerth (son of).

Llywelyn Fawr married the daughter of King John (1199 – 1216) in an effort to unite the two countries. However, the idea was not a success and border wars were to continue between England and Wales into the thirteenth century. He played an influential part in drawing up the Magna-Carta in 1215 AD, obtained recognition, and concessions for Wales and it is believed built Castell-y-Bere in 1221 AD.

Sara Eade Collection

Dysynini Valley

Sara Eade Collection

Castell y Bere

Llywelyn the Great died in 1240 AD leaving two sons, David who was half English on his Royal mother's side, and Griffith. The two brothers disagreed on how Wales should be governed. Eventually Griffith was put into detention and later imprisoned in the Tower of London. He was killed in an escape bid. This untimely death led David into war with the English, for Griffith was popular with his countrymen and his death caused unrest. Wales now faced a period of hardship and misery never before experienced. David died in 1246 AD leaving the Welsh throne vacant.

Peace was again shattered when land in Wales, the four Cantrefs (districts, hundreds, in Welsh cantref = 100 trefs) was misappropriated and given to Prince Edward. The people called upon Llywelyn for help and conflict once again broke out. In the following ten years Llywelyn became the symbol of freedom and to win many battles. In 1267 AD after another abortive venture into Wales the King and Llywelyn made peace. Llywelyn was given back his lands and was made Prince of Wales.

In 1272 AD Edward I came to the English throne, and from then onwards events got progressively worse for Prince Llywelyn who had refused to pay homage to the new King.

The future bride of the Prince, Eleanor, was captured at sea and became the King's prisoner. Edward used her to lure Llywelyn to court, but to no avail.

The King was not to be slighted so he called upon his Barons to bring the Welsh Prince to submission. In 1277 he set about a campaign with soldierly skill which was carefully and coldly devised.

His army was mainly made up of Welsh levies from Gwent and Glamorgan, English raised by Feudal levy and regular mercenaries from Gascony. The mailed cavalry who had been dominant since the fifth century were to become obsolete by a form of infantry raised from the common people. The traditional weapons of the axe, club, spear and sword were to be out classed by the dramatic ascendency of the long bow. It was in this sphere that the men of South Wales excelled with astonishing efficiency.

There is a record of a Knight being struck by an arrow which pierced his mailed shirt, mailed breeches, thigh, wooden saddle and finally buried itself deeply into the horses' flank. The efficiency, accuracy, rate of fire and range has only been replaced by the development of the modern rifle.

War once again rocked Wales, Edward sending three large armies into the Principality. David, Prince Llywelyn's younger brother sided with the King and as a reward was made an English Baron, and given part of Snowdonia to rule over. The antagonists eventually made peace and Llywelyn married his bride Eleanor in Worcester Cathedral in 1277 AD.

Five years of uneasy peace were to follow, but in 1282 AD David took up arms against the King, and inevitably Prince Llywelen became involved in the conflict.

With military skill Edward sent an army through the centre of Wales, dividing North from South. At the same time another army advanced across the Northern coastal region. The King's fleet blockaded Anglesey cutting off supplies of corn and prevented food supplies reaching Llywelyn's forces in Snowdonia.

The Prince successfully prevented the invasion of Anglesey and losses sustained by the King's forces gave temporary respite to Llywelen who then moved South to recruit more men leaving David to guard the mountain passes of Snowdonia.

Prince Llywelyn recruited a large army, and went to Builth to meet local nobility. It was his intention to secure the pass that linked the North with the South. Leaving the main body of his army on a mountain overlooking the River Wye, he posted a detachment to guard Pont Oerwyn, a river crossing. The English ,helped by local Welsh, attacked the defenders from both sides. The Prince, hurrying back from what could have been a treacherous parley was intercepted by an English Knight, Stephen Frankton (or Adam de Franction), and killed in the ensuing fight. Prince Llywelyn's head was severed from his body, and sent to the King at Conway where it was put on display. One third of the Welsh forces, two thousand men, were killed.

On hearing the news, David claimed the title of Prince of Wales. His ventures appear to be linked with Castell y Bere ('Bere' in Welsh indicating Bird of Prey).

The Castle, or Castell was built by Llywelyn the Great about 1221 AD. It was one of the few Castles that was truly Welsh and equalled any that had been constructed by the Norman/English up to that date. It was strategically positioned upon a rocky outcrop in what was at one time an estuary, and may have possibly been surrounded by marshy ground. It guarded what would have been in those days the approach to several important passes through the mountains to Dolgellau and Machynlleth.

How the castle might have looked; taken from a display board close to the castle

It is believed that a signal post was placed upon Craig yr Aderyn (Bird Rock). Flags were used to warn the Castle defenders of approaching danger, possibly from the direction of the sea. Edward I used his fleet to good effect to maintain his stranglehold upon Wales.

Castell y Bere came under siege in April 1283 AD by William de Valence, the Earl of Pembroke, and it fell in the same month. David (Dafydd in Welsh) was now a fugitive and organised resistance begun to crumble. He took refuge in Snowdonia hiding with his family in a cave. He was betrayed by one of his countrymen in whom he had put his trust, was hunted down and captured. David was despised by Edward I for his betrayal of both the English and the Welsh.

The crown had recognised his services by making him an English Baron but he did little to help Prince Llywelyn's cause when his countrymen needed him. Edward had David taken to Shrewsbury where he was dragged through the streets, and finally hanged, drawn and quartered.

Castell y Bere was committed into the custody of Robert Fitzwalter who at the same time was granted the liberty of hunting all kinds of wild beasts in the country. During the occupation in 1283 some refortifications were carried out at a cost of £262 5s 10¾d and in 1285 'Bere' was given borough status. A new town being developed on the plateau to the east, where it could have given some additional defence to the area and with the encouragement of English settlers and business interests would have formed some kind of economic hold upon the area.

These boroughs were to remain alien to the Welsh countryside and were disliked by the Welsh people. Edward embarked upon his castle building campaign to surround Wales.

The uprising in 1294 AD was led by Madog-ap-Llywelyn, the son of an ancient and dispossessed Merioneth family. It was timed to take place on September 30th when Edward I intended to send his combined English and Welsh forces to the Continent to fight the French.

Castell y Bere, Denbigh and Caernarvon were attached and the latter captured and destroyed.

Some of the King's army had already sailed to France. However, with his remaining forces he moved into North Wales with remarkable speed. By Christmas he was at Aberconway. In January 1295 AD he moved towards Bangor and whilst his baggage train was strung out along the road it was brilliantly ambushed. This sortie put an end to the King's Winter Campaign.

Madog moved south raiding Oswestry and Shrewsbury. He was pursued across the border by the Earl of Warwick and the two armies clashed on March 5th on the small plain of Maes-Moydog near Castle Caereinion, Montgomeryshire. The English carried out a most successful attack, winning the day and effectively putting an end to Welsh resistance.

Whether the Welsh were to become reconciled to English rule it is hard to say. However, shortly after this event Edward I attached Scotland in an effort to unify these Islands. He used an army of six thousand well organised soldiers, four thousand of these were Welsh.

Using the same tactics that defeated Madog they were to rout the Scots.

What eventually happened to the English defenders of Castell y Bere is not known. However, excavations have revealed a quantity of burnt timber which would indicate that the Castle was destroyed, or at least severely damaged. Bere now fades into obscurity until a mention of an episode in the mid fifteenth century linking one Dafydd Gough (Coch-y-Pennant, Red of that name) who defended the Castle. In sixteenth century writings it is referred to as a "large strong building which is now destroyed and cast to the ground".

DRAWING

1 The approach leading to the Castle is by a footpath from the car park. This passes over the defence ditches and pit.

2 Site of drawbridge

3 Gateway guarded by the Barbican (outwork defending a drawbridge), Round Tower and Middle Tower.

4 Courtyard, an irregular triangular shape with towers located near the corners.

5 Well, originally fifteen feet deep. The site of some interesting finds.

6 Out buildings sited in the courtyard. Date of construction is uncertain. They could have been used by the occupant in the 15th century or they may have been workshops, stables, bakehouse or kitchen. In early castles these buildings were often sited in the courtyard.

7 Sally – Port, a gateway through which a garrison could launch an attack, or a place giving a means of escape.

8 Staircase, leading to the upper floor of the North Tower the end of which is semi-circular.

9 North Tower, believed to have contained the Chapel on the upper floor because of the elaborate stone sculpture found there.

10 Middle Tower, a Keep-type building.

11 Yard, secondary walls built during the English occupation to link South Tower with the main castle.

12 South Tower, probably made up of private apartments, including a garderobe (lavatory) .

The South Tower guards the southern approach up the valley.

The Castle was placed in the care of Cadw: Welsh Historic Monuments in 1949.

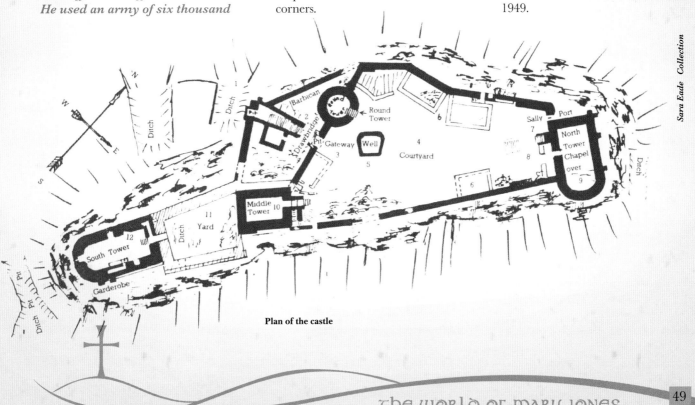

Sara Eade Collection

Plan of the castle

Map of Merionethshire showing Ystumer

Sara Eade Collection

The following was a paper read out at a meeting of the Towyn Debating Society held in March 1886.

The meaning of the word Ystumaner is the 'shape of a heifer' because upon crossing the bridge over the River Dysynni near Caerberllan from the parish of Llanfihangel y Pennant, the view of that part of Ystumaner visible from this point resemble a heifer. The bridge also bears this name. The Petty Sessional District which includes Towyn, Aberdovey, Pennal and part of the parish of Talyllyn is known by this name. Tradition transmitted from bye-gone times says that the High Functionary who fixed the boundaries of the Petty Session division of the country first beheld this fair part of the land from where it seems to resemble a heifer. I will not tell a tale many times told, nor shall I attempt to walk the beaten track of the historians. Abler pens than mine have made careful records of the noted places in the district – St Cadvan's Church, Ynysymaengwyn, Grufydd ap Adda and Owen Law Goch etc have had their share of attention. It is therefore intended that this short paper should recite the result of my gleanings from the old people who have gone to where day and night never succeed one another, and where the poor owner of Nantmynawydd has found a refuge from the tyrant of Caerberllan.

Nantmynawydd and Caerberllan are on the boundary of Ystumaner, and the tale has such a close connection with the bridge that gives the district its name that so small a digression, will, it is hoped, be pardoned. Caerbellan Mansion and estate were important in the time of good Queen Bess, but the proud owner of them coveted the vineyard of a poor man who lived at Nantmynawydd, which means the coveted dingle. Nothing would satisfy him but getting possession of this quiet nook. Having failed to obtain his object by fair means, he resorted to foul ones, as was very common in those days. He had a beautiful fawn; this he caused to be, one night, placed in the poor man's barn and in the morning he ordered his retainers to search the country for it with the result of course of finding it where it had been put. Theft was then a capital crime. The option was given this poor man of choosing between the farm and his life. He chose the latter, which he ransomed with his farm. In time this poor man came to die, and before he died, he added a wish, or as some people would call a curse, of which the following is a rendering I have heard.

St Cadfans Church after remodelling between 1881-1884

Sara Eade Collection

Interior of St Cadfans Church before remodelling between 1881-1884

Sara Eade Collection

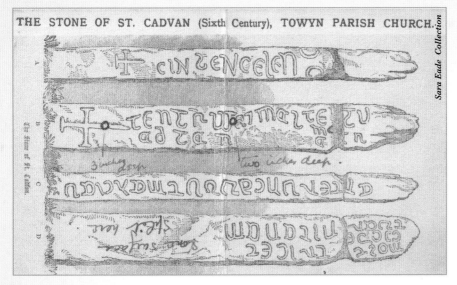

THE STONE OF ST. CADVAN (Sixth Century), TOWYN PARISH CHURCH.

Sara Eade Collection

inconspicuous among them stand the names of Shaw of Shrewsbury, Gaskell Phillips, Dewi ap Dewi, Francis Jones and a host of others, some of whom have killed Salmon weighing from 30 to 40 pounds. Following the river hurriedly, and passing on the opposite bank, Talybont of Royal celebrity and "Tomen Ddrainog" the weir of Ynys y Maengwyn is reached. This fish trap was preserved in spite of all remonstrances until it was made useless by law in 1850. There, within the memory of the writer, stood a cottage and a round house for curing fish. One named Philip Evans of Pensarn and others had long and fruitless struggles with the Squires of Ynys-y-Maengwyn on account of the wholesale slaughtering of fish in this place.

'Tra bydd haul yn troi yn yr entrych, ac y rhed dwr dan bont Ystumaner, bydded I aerod Caerbellan fod mor wirion am both peth ac ydwrf fi am y cyw carw'

Which means – While the sun revolves in the firmament, and while water runs under the bridge of Ystumaner let the heirs of Caerbellan be as mad as I am innocent of how the fawn got into my barn.

The curse fell upon the heirs, and there was a succession of mad heirs, that is, they became mad on entering into possession. The Estate was ultimately sold because of the inability of the heirs to manage it. The bridge of Ystumaner has been left, and glance taken of the broad valley known as Bird Rock. The home of the Cormorants, and the harbour of a wonderful echo. From this point a grand view of the River Dysynni in all the majesty of its zig zag course is obtained.

Ynysmaengwyn in its heyday

Sara Eade Collection

Opposite the mansion of Peniarth the remains of a fish-weir are still to be seen, but to the credit of the Wynne family be it said, that this unsportsmanlike manner of killing fish was done away with, before that became compulsory by law. It would be interesting to dwell on the banks of the slow and deep flowing river, and record the variant deeds of many Knights of the fin, not

Near here is Dolffrowd or Blood Meadow, where a sanguinary conflict took place between the Ancient Britons and the Romans, the former occupying the Fort of Bryn Castell and the latter the Roman fort now known as "Tomen Ddraenog". When this meadow was drained about 1862 many fragments of implements of war were found, which corroborated the tradition preserved by the Country people. Ynys-y-Maengwyn, the abode of Madam Owen whose name is blended with the history of the estate in its most eventful time. She built the new parts of the Mansion facing East and West in the year 1720 and had all the stones, which are dressed, brought there, if tradition be true, at the expense of her tenants, from a

Sara Eade

All that remains of the great Mansion of Ynysmaengwyn. This doorway was part of the section built by Ann Owen.

Sara Eade

Dovecote and workshops of the old Ynysmaengwyn estate

quarry on Moel Caethle. She effected many improvements on the estate, by building etc and was careful to have the fact recorded by memorial stones and otherwise. She also built and endowed the Alms Houses at Towyn, principally in order to provide a home for her maid, in the year 1738. "This Alms House was built by Ann Owen of Ynys-y-Maengwyn, Widd. In 1738". This is a true copy of the inscription on the Alms Houses. The head of a Whale, a Raven, and a Lion Rampant, are engraved on a stone above the inscription, anyhow so it was in Dec. 1787. When an exchange was made in 1882, whereby better buildings were secured to the poor, the stone was removed and has since been a dispute between Mr John Corbett of Ynys-y-Maengwyn and Mr R G Price one of the Trustees of the Charity. The houses have been the refuge of generations of five old widows ever since, and the endowment, thanks to the vigilance of Mr W R Davies, Solicitor, Vestry Clerk to the Parish of Towyn, was at the time of the Ynysymaengwyn Estate saved from what I call it, confiscation. Madam Ann Owen, I guess, would have turned in her grave, if the hand of the spoiler had deprived these helpless old women of their means of sustenance.

Madam Owen was a masculine sort of body, she often signed the minutes of the Parish Vestry as Ann Owen, Chairman, and was present at many Vestries, when no small quantity of good old beer was consumed, which was the custom in those days. Ann Owen was present at a Vestry meeting held on the 4th July 1738, when the church wardens and Overseers were empowered to proceed in the recovery of the Charity known as the Lewis Lloyd's Charity. The following is a copy of the minute:

> *"Since Mrs Elizabeth Vaughan, Penmaen, Relic of Mr Lewis Vaughan deceased, was not pleased to return a satisfactory answer to the proposals of the last Vestry, in relation to the gift of Mr Lewis Lloyd to the Poor of Parsel Isyrafon we whose names are hereunto subscribed do hereby empower the churchwardens and Overseers of the Poor of the said Parish of Towyn to proceed in the recovery of the said Charity at the Law District."*

Lewis Lloyd's Charity, which really means Abergroes Farm, has been preserved for the Parish. As time went on the poor died out of Parsel Is yr afon, and Lewis Vaughan of Penmaen appropriated the money for his own use. He was one of the Trustees. Hence the proceedings ordered to be taken by the Vestry. It appears that the rent of the farm was subsequently paid to the Overseers of the Poor of the Parish, who applied it in aid of the Poor Rate. This was however prevented by the Charity Commissioners, who prepared a scheme by which it was given in aid of Education, and since the year 1862 a sum of money about Nineteen pounds a year has been paid in support of each of the following schools – Pennal, Aberdovey and Towyn National School.

The Parish of Towyn has many Charities, an account of which was painted on a Board hung up in St Cadvan's Church, which has been removed. I know not where.

Sara Eade Collection

College Green Towyn

An account of these Charities are given overleaf. (Below)

By Whom Given	Date	Purpose
1 Vincent Corbet, Anne Owen, Mrs Hall and Ann Pugh	Unknown	To the poor
2 Vincent Corbet	1717	Free school in Village of Towyn
3 Lady Mayor of London	1717	For teaching 24 poor children in the Parish of Towyn
4 Ann Owen Alms Houses already mentioned		
5 The Rev Mr Morgan	1739	To men, women and children for repeating the Church Catechism
6 Lewis Lloyd	1691	Already described
7 Richard Jones	unknown	To the poor of the two townships of the said parish called Dauddyffryn and Cefnrhosissaf
8 David Evans	unknown	To the poor of the township of Cynfalfawr in the said parish
9 David Hugh	unknown	"
10 Owen Humphreys' daughter	unknown	To the poor

Charities 3 and 6 are now applied in aid of Education.

Ann Owen's Charity to the Almshouses is applied as directed by the donor. I have no means of ascertaining what has become of the others, but would be glad if circumstances permitted a search after them.

Ynysmaengwyn Estate passed from Ann Owen to Harry Corbet, the younger son of her daughter. Edward, the elder brother having displeased the old dame by his profligate habits and at one time having called her an 'Old Bitch'. Harry Corbet was known as 'Corbet the Good'. He was fond of prayer, was generous to the poor, a good landlord and a kind neighbour. He used to cultivate a quantity of land, one half of the produce of which he gave to the poor. There were secluded spots in the shrubberies red with the marks of kneeling, where he used to retire to commune with his God. He had to do so in private, because his wife did not approve of his devotional habits. After living at Ynys for about eight years, and proving a blessing to the country, he sickened, and when approaching death, his wife, a proud, vain women, fearing she would be turned from Ynys, took him away in a Chaise and he died on the road to or at Machynlleth.

Edward Corbet, his older brother, succeeded him. The history of this noted man would take up more time than I have at my disposal this evening so I must

Sara Eade Collection

Raven detail from the Lodge by the gates of the old Ynysmaengwyn estate

summarise. On his advent to the country he found it particularly deficient in the knowledge of Medicine and Surgery, and he sent for a Medical man from London to instruct him in those important branches of knowledge, and such was his natural aptitude for learning that in a short time he became highly proficient in medicine and skilled in surgery, and to his everlasting credit be it recorded that he sought out the cause he knew not, and dispensed physic and advice with a free hand and a willing heart wherever he found suffering and want. He was a great sportsman himself, and wished all his tenants and dependants to partake in his favourite pastimes, and it was a rule that all wild birds shot on the then vast estate should be bought at the Mansion unless they could be disposed of to greater advantage elsewhere. He was fond of horse-racing and at one time had sixty race horses in his stables. He bought all the Oats produced on the estate. The Towyn races lasted for a whole week and people came from all parts of the country between Chester, Shrewsbury and Hereford. The Racecourse was on Morfa Towyn farm, and many people living remember the course and the Grand Stand and for that matter the races. Racing was a distinguished characteristic of Towyn and helped to make it known all over the Country.

from Geg-y-ffos to Gwalia such as the late Griffith Jones, his brother Hugh, Francis Jones the Tailor father to our distinguished townsman Mr J Ff Jones, Frankwell Hall.

The marches from Pall Mall and Ynys las to the sea were all common land, teaming with wild fowl of every description, forming a very heaven to the sportsman. It was also the poor man's estate. Every head of a family in the place, had a cow and more than three acres of land, or a pair of donkeys, flocks of geese, ducks etc. The inhabitants had the right of cutting peat for burning, so in reality the marsh, wide open and free was a source of almost inexhaustible supply of food, fuel and recreation to the people; which no doubt accounted for their robust health, independence of character and excellence in all athletic sports. The idea of draining the source of such manliness was conceived, and after a while, one called Jackson, hit upon a stratagem which unfortunately was successfully

carried out, and Edward Corbet was deceived into lending his powerful influence to the fell work.

Jackson announced by means of song and trumpet that coal of good quality had been discovered in abundance at Bronbiban. A feast to celebrate the event was given at Ynys-y-maengwyn, and Mr Corbet in the exuberance of his credulity promised coal to all the inhabitants of the township of Faenol, if they would give up their common rights. All the adjoining landowners, hungry for their shares urged the poor people to assent, and they assented. In 1805 an Act of Parliament was passed entitled – "An Act for enclosing, embanking, draining and improving certain lands in the Township of Vaenol in the Parish of Towyn, in the County of Merioneth, made in the 45th year of the reign of King George 3rd, ie 1805" allotting to each greedy land grubber his share of the spoil, is now in a good state of preservation amongst the parochial documents of this Parish.

Elephant detail from the gates by the gates of the old Ynysmaengwyn estate

Sara Eade Collection

Sara Eade

When Edward Corbet was at the Zenith of his power, Towyn was a harbour, or it may not inappropriately be called a seaport, because the tide did ebb and flow at Gwalia. Ships not only came there, but there was a shipbuilding yard on the eastern bank of Pill ditch, opposite where subsequently The Calvinistic Methodist built a chapel. The ship carpenters of Towyn noted for their skill and the youth of the place were renowned for swimming. Some in this room are old enough to remember many of those who learnt to swim by floating with the tide,

An Evergreen Oak Tree, a rare tree still on the Ynysmaengwyn estate

Towyn-on-Sea

Sara Eade Collection

There was no coal found at Bronbiban, but it is only fair to the character of Edward Corbet to say, that he believed implicitly in the reports made to him and that he was deceived as much as anyone on this point. But if there had been coal, there was no formal and written arrangements made whereby the inhabitants were given title to get and carry away free of charge, coal for their use. This was possibly, an omission on the part of the public functionaries of the time, as well as a deep plot on the part of those who deprived the inhabitants of their grand inheritance. The glittering picture proved too tempting, and the reality parted with for the shadow.

Frankwell Street, Towyn.

Sara Eade Collection

Frankwell St Towyn

Sara Eade Collection

A bit of old Towyn

It might not be much out of place, to warn the present inhabitants of Towyn to consider well before they part with the small, but important remnant of the vast common land, which is yet in their possession. It is evident, that Jack O'Lantern promises cost Towyn dearly in the past, and there are no reliable proofs or securities, that the present generation will not fall into the same pit, if they follow the same phantom. The lands were allotted in 1809, and in a short time enclosed. It was

about this time that the Embankment known as 'Clawdd Swnd' was constructed, which prevented the tide from coming to Gwalia. When engaged on this work the men wrote the famous round letter (Round Robin) or 'Llythyr Crwn' to Edward Corbet, asking for an increase in wages. This is the first instance of combination among workmen known of in this part of the country. The difficulty of keeping the leaders from falling under, or incurring the displeasure of the Squire, was a matter of importance, so this happy thought was hit upon, and succeeded, and secured not only an increase of wages but the approval of the Squire, partly, no doubt, because of the ingenuity of the device. The idea is supposed to have been conceived by Evan Shon y Gardnar. A man noted for sagacity.

The origin of Calvinistic Methodism, and the hostility of Edward Corbet to the sect, has been recorded, I dare say, so I shall pass over it briefly.

Jones Mathafarn, preached on Pen-y-bryn Mawr, and the Huntsman brought a pack of Fox-hounds there, with the intention of getting them to howl and bark, and so prevent the service from being conducted, but to his surprise, when he gave the usual signal, not a bark was uttered, and the

dogs, which had never disobeyed him before refused obedience and crouched and trembled at his heels. The Huntsman was so impressed with the behaviour of the dogs, that he went home and told his master that he would never attempt to disturb a meeting of Methodists again.

The father of Methodism in the place was Edward Williams, father of the late Benjamin Williams and Grandfather of the wife of Mr Thomas Smith of Gwalia. When this good old man was going around the town one day, with a bell in his hand, announcing that a meeting would be held, Mr Corbet met him, took the bell from his hand and struck him with it on one of his cheeks. Edward Williams offered him the other cheek, saying "my blood which you have shed, will rise up in judgement against you." He did not strike him again. Edward Williams was offered the means to prosecute but this he positively declined, saying he would leave vengeance to his Master.

The River Dysynni, with its trade in lime, stone etc etc, deserves further mention. Many kilns formerly stood on its banks; one as high up as Cilcemaes, another at Talybont, which is still standing, another at Rhydygarnedd and another at Tonfanau.

Sara Eade Collection

Corbett Arms Hotel

Shipping by small craft was briskly carried on. There are people now residing in Towyn who remember a ship being built near Rhydygarnedd named' Deborah' and commanded by Capt Evan Davies from Bryn.

The fishing of the river was free from the 'Agoriad', 'Gored', 'Cewyll' or Weir to the sea and afforded occupation to half a dozen boats and twenty to thirty sturdy people. Then fishing was also unrestricted, and was carried on at all time, except when it would be too cold to draw the nets, and when the fish would be heavy with spawn. There was an abundance of fish, not only for the nets but for the anglers also. Those who were intimately acquainted with the state of things at the time restrictive laws were first passed, maintain that a marked decrease in the number of fish coming up the river took place, when, what is by a great number of people considered as iniquitous laws, were passed. These notions are held be people in all parts of the country.

Towyn prior to 1850 was the haunt of noted anglers, who came from all parts of the country, and found at the Corbet Arms Hotel, accommodation second to none in the principality for comfort. Mr Owen Owen, the landlord of this Hostelry, was a champion Harpist, and accompanied Mr Edward Corbet on his periodical visits to London, and was there ranked amongst the most proficient harpists of the time. There is an oil painting of this faithful man on the grand staircase at Ynysymaengwyn.

Mr Corbet had obtained separation or was separated from his wife. There happened to be a banquet at Ynys on the day when news of Mrs Corbet's death was received. It had been arranged for the old Harpist to attend the feast as usual, but when he was requested to play, he said to his master, for the first time – "No Sir. I cannot play on this instrument, the gift of Mrs Corbet (kissing the Harp while speaking), while she, who loved you till death, and whom I shall revere till my death is lying dead awaiting burial."

Towyn was noted for its Harpists, Pennillion Singers and dancers – the Jones family, 'Bryd y clychau Bach' have been from time immemorial to the present day, renowned for their pennillion singing and dancing to the music of the harp. I cannot dwell on this theme, sweet as it is to my pen. And may only mention the names of Richard Humffre, Telyniwr, Rhys Owen, the generous neighbour, cockfighter, Churchwarden and Constable; Ephraim y Felyn, the Champion football player, cock and bull fighter; Hugh Rowland, Pennal and scores of others that might be mentioned as prominent members of the 'Noswaith Lawen Geiniog', and institution somewhat resembling the modern 'Penny Readings' but more given to the song and the dance, and Rustic Drama called 'Interlude' or 'Anterlute'.

The Superstitions of Ystumaner
The fairy tales of Llyn Barfog have been so often and well told, that I will not repeat them.

There was much beauty and fascination in some of the superstitions of our fore-

fathers. I have had the pleasure on conversing face to face, in the halcyon days of my youth, with people who honestly and sincerely believed that the Rosemary blossomed, that the yoked oxen knelt and that the bees swarmed on old Christmas nights, which they believed was the right date of the birth of the Redeemer of mankind. There also existed, and does yet exist, a strong belief in dreams. The recital of some of which I honestly confess, has often perplexed me. The following are some instances:

Years before the marshes below Gwyddelfynydd and Cilcemmas were allotted, Joseph Andrew, a truthful , upright man, saw in a dream the whole allotment laid out, and the ditches which afterwards separated them out. The man was so impressed by the dream, that he told his wife and others, and actually pointed out to them the courses of the ditches, site of bridges etc. When years afterwards the survey of the marshes was made, and a plan of the drainage laid out, people were astonished to find everything done according to Joseph Andrew's dream. He also saw in a dream the ship 'Alliance' commanded by Capt Richard Humphreys, under full sail in "Llyn y Gored". This he told his family at breakfast and in a few hours the news came that Captain Humphreys' son had lost his life at the very spot where the dreamer had seen the ship.

There was also, and still is, a strong unswerving belief in the appearance of ghosts. Ynys-y-maengwyn had more than one. Conspicuous amongst them was the 'Lady Ghost of John's Well', or as most of

the country people called the spirit "Lady Wen y Gat ganol". The spectre was to be seen walking, beautifully attired in rustling silk, but always wearing a look of unutterable grief and melancholy. The comely phantom still goes her rounds for all that is known. "None but the brave deserve the fair", and no-one brave enough has been found to induce this sorrow laden spirit to divulge the cause of her midnight wanderings. At times she would look through the window, into the banqueting hall, and the sight of the black eues and handsome white faces would silence the sound of revelry.

The other most prominent denizen of the nether world was the 'Butler's Ghost' of the long corridor. This spirit finds occupation in walking along the passage connecting the old and the new parts of the mansion, and the echo of his footsteps are heard all over the house. Many tales are told of his freaks and antics which I must not repeat tonight.

About the year 1816 a man was stealing apples from Botalog garden and was shot by the gardener; the wounded man crawled up one of the sidewalks to the middle, and then fell exhausted from loss of blood, and before assistance was rendered to him a big patch of ground was made crimson with his blood. He was removed to the Greenhouse where he died. The stains remained, and in time, Mr Scott, who resided at Bodtalog, had the paths dug, and the earth removed and the surface gravelled, but the blood would not be hidden, and is spite of everything that could be done, the blood kept reappearing every spring and autumn, crying according to the belief of the many, for vengeance against the murderer, for it is alleged that the Gardener's sons shot the man, not the Gardener.

The ghost stories, stored in my memory, would take too long a time to tell, even if you had the patience to listen to them.

The ghost which used to drive a pair of Grey Horses in Happy Valley.
The "Flaming Ghost" of Gwyddgwion
The "Mischievious Ghost" of Penhelig
And the "Spinning Ghost" of Caethle can have none of their feats recited.

Happy Valley

The achievements of the Conjuror, or wise man, or "Gwr Cyfarwydd" or rather the Wizard cannot be enumerated. The belief that some men possess the power, by performing mystic rites of holding conversation with the spiritual beings, who are conversant with the past, present and future of mankind, was strong in recent times and is not dead yet. Men followed the profession of a Conjuror openly, and were treated with much respect and reverence. Their chief work was to undo the evil wrought by witches. This form of superstition had strong hold on people within my memory. I well remember several instances of wonderful cure of persons, cattle and horses ascribed to the 'Wise Man'. People would travel a long way to a conjuror, and would pay him well. Do not imagine that this has reference to the dark ages. There are many people living who have sought the help of the power of darkness to do what members of the Medical Profession has failed to do, and I am not too sure that this is not done in the Parish of Towyn up to this very day.

Celebrities

St Cadvan, Gryffydd ap Adda, Ieuen Brydydd Hir, Dafydd Ionawr, Dr William Owen Pughe, Tanybryn, noted as they were must be passed without remark, as their deed are chronicled in the books of other prophets.

Edward William, Father of Methodism and the fighting preachers, who were refused for love or money, a passage over the Dysynni then took a boat themselves and were followed by the ferrymen, who struck two of them with impunity, and when they, the ferrymen, came to the third, he said "my friends, you have struck two cheeks, which is the maximum liberty given you by the Gospel" and thereon he turned upon them and thrashed them soundly. The ferrymen were civil to preachers for the rest of their days.

1800-1835 John Jones of Penparc as the founder of elementary education in the district deserves a prominent place in the records of the locality. I have nothing at hand to tell me of his early career, but have often been told of his proficiency and severity as a Teacher. He kept school at Bryncrug, and had pupils from all the surrounding district. He was famous for his knowledge of navigation, and had

Penhelig Aberdovey

sailors at his school from all the ports between Portmadoc and Aberystwyth. John Jones was fond of corporal punishment and was known to have at least hastened the death of more than one of his pupils, but he made the place distinguished for learning.

Talgarth

Aberdovey

There were contemporaneously with John Jones, ladies keeping Lady's schools. The Misses Vaughan at Pennal and the Misses Scott at Penhelig, Aberdovey. The young ladies from the higher class of the surrounding district received their training at these places.

1830-1852 John Thomas, the National SchoolMaster at Towyn, was a man of a different stamp. He used to teach instrumental music to his pupils, and his school was noted for the excellence of its penmanship and arithmetic. John Thomas was a luxurious, and would smoke in the schoolroom, fry, and cat cockles, drink a goodly quantity of beer and fall asleep. He taught most of his pupils to smoke, by sending them out to light his pipe – this was before the days of the Lucifer Matches. There are many in Towyn today that learned his habit from this practice. John Thomas often called the scholars by name than otherwise. Many people are known by those names to this day, such as "Twm y Llymri cer", "Wilcat", "Ned y blunt", "Ysbryd milgi", and "Bwbi Dunce" etc etc

When the history of education in the place comes to be written fully, the names of the following gentlemen will occupy prominent places – the late Mr C F Thruston of Talgarth, founder of the Pennal Bristish School, Mr R Price of Dolaugwyn, founder of the Bryncrug School; Mr W W Jones, ("Gwilym o Fon") founder of the Towyn British School, and Mr Edwin Jones as the first to provide the district with the means of Higher Education.

Mail Carriers

50 years ago, the letter bags were carried by a woman between Towyn and Machynlleth. Shoned Edwards, late wife of Edward Edwards, Royal Marines, performed the astounding feat of walking to and from Machynlleth through Happy Valley every day, except Sundays, for 15 years. She would go to Machynlleth through Happy Valley, and return through Aberdovey – a distance of 26 miles and would often carry a heavy burden. This would, I think. Compare favourably with the walking exploits of Western the Champion pedestrian. Just think, a woman walking a 156 miles a week or 8,112 miles a year.

In those days it took over a week for a letter to travel from London to Towyn. After Shoned's performance, letters were carried by Shon Matha in a cart and afterwards by William and Humphrey Williams on horseback. Then came the Mail Cart with David Lloyd on the summit of it and later

Mail courier & wagon, the postmen was William Rowlands who lived at Abergynolwyn

still 'Y Goits fawr' ie The Mail Coach and four, and twenty years ago by train, when the seclusion of Towyn was finally and fully ruined. Towyn was formerly a thrifty place; the people doing all manner of things, in order to help the ordinary way of wage earning – such as cutting peat on the shore for burning, -Tori mawn y mor; 'Pabwyra', that is gathering rushes, peeling them and dipping them into melted fat to make a candle. Straw plaiting was also carried on extensively. Hats, and many sorts of fancy baskets were made which commanded a ready sale at remunerative prices. Wool factories, employing a considerable number of hands, were within thirty years, in full operation at Pandy, Perthyctia and Rhydyronen. Weaving by hand loom, afforded employment to a large number of people. The sound of a Weaver's shuttle could be heard at almost every other door in some streets of Towyn quite recently.

Lead mining at Melin Llyn Pair and

Cottages at Melin Llyn Pair

Tyddyn-y-briddell, and copper mining on Mynydd bychan above Aberdovey was not long since an important industry. There are levels made by the Romans, running under Pant-y-Cae near Melin Llyn Pair. Herring fishing was followed much more regularly, and on a much greater scale than lately, as late as 1840. There were ten boats engaged in the trade – noted amongst them were the 'Ocean Chief', the 'Cormorant', the

'Jonah', the 'Antelope' etc etc. Some 130 years ago a terrible disaster overtook the fishing boats in Cardigan Bay, which on a certain night in Autumn was full of boats, when a fearful storm of wind came from the East and 120 boats were wrecked. There were scores of them to be seen the following morning floating keel upwards. That night, 50 wives were made widows at Borth. At that time boats came fishing to this bay from all the ports on the coast, hence the enormous loss of life.

I find that I have drawn my plan on too big a scale to be carried out and must therefore only mention a large number of things, which I should like to describe in detail, such as Brothwell, the wild Irishman who lost the Caethle Estate by daring to take possession of a wreck on the shore.

Charles William Semies, the Dutchman, who married the heiress of Bodtalog, and who took her away to a foreign land with the intention of murdering her, and how she was saved by the intervention of Mr Scot, Equerry to King George IV, and how subsequently Mr Scot married the heiress and became the owner of Bodtalog.

Talgarth, one of the most important places in the district must be omitted so must Penhelig, Gogarth, Dyffryngwyn, Bron-y-prys and even Dolaugwyn can have but a passing glance.

Lead Mines - Melin Llyn Pair in Happy Valley

Marine promenade and beach at Towyn

Sara Eade Collection

The Sands, Towyn

When the Victorious Army of Oliver Cromwell was marching through the country, desolating as it went, the owner of Dolaugwyn went forth to meet the victors with presents, which consisted among other things of two white oxen, which were accepted, as was the invitation to a feast. Dolaugwyn was thus spared, while so many other places were destroyed.

The state of the marshes between Towyn and Aberdovey was very different prior to 1862 to what it is now. There was a big pool below Penllyn, extending as far as Glaywern, upon which I spent many days boating. The Caethle Brook and Llyn y Borth were the best trout waters in the country before the Melinllynpair Mining Company, began in 1851 to pollute them with lead washings, and fill up the bed of the brook with refuse, which proved, not only deadly to the fish, but also to ducks, geese and horses. These marshes, as well as the marshes of the Dysynni Valley were scientifically drained in 1862. The Dovey Marshes at a cost of about £7,000 and the Dysynni Marshes at a cost of £30,000.

The sound of a railway locomotive was first re-echoed by the hills and vales of the district about the same time as the marshes were drained. On the advent of these changes, and I call them changes advisedly, the charming seclusion, the primitive habits of the inhabitants, the wild fowl and the ague disappeared.

The history of Towyn will never be satisfactorily written, unless the prominent part of their spheres, played by the following people be incorporated in it.

Peter-y-Pandy. Skilful of hand and ready of tongue

Ellis y Maes Coch. The Classical Scholar, Pigman and Cowman.

John O'Benbryn. The eccentric soldier, mason and gardener.

Francis y Clochydd, his devotion to the fabric and doctrine of the church.

Ap Ieuan, Tymawr, Farmer, Poet and Divine.

Davies O'Bennal, Incumbent of Pennal, noted Scholar and pedestrian.

Hugh Jones. Y Pregethwr Methodist.

Hugh Lloyd. The Independent.

Jack Roger. The Wesleyan.

Thomas Beddoes. The road-maker, and builder of Bryn-y-Mor.

John Hughes. The Railway Contractor and builder of Neptune Hall etc

William Parry. The host of the Corbet Arms Hotel, and Churchwarden for 40 years.

Dr John Pughe (Ioan ap yr hen feddyg) of Aberdovey. The skilful Surgeon, Antiquarian, Preacher, Botanist and Historian.

Thomas Edwards. 40 years Vestry Clerk and for many years Clerk to the Local Board and always the generous friend of the poor.

And last but by no means least,

Evan Newall. Farmer, Merchant, Founder of the Presbyterian cause and of the Market Hall, Builder of the People's Market House, Caethle Mill, Restorer of Bodtalog Mansion, reclaimer of the marshes, the terror of Tyrants and the unswerving friend of the oppressed.

This paper was found amongst the papers of Richard Oswald Griffiths when he died and it is believed that it was given to his father Hugh William Griffiths. Permission to reproduce it here was given by Hugh's grandson, Richard Wynne Griffiths.

Sara Eade Collection

TOWYN. CORBETT & RAVEN HOTEL.
Corbett Arms Hotel and view up the Fathew Valley

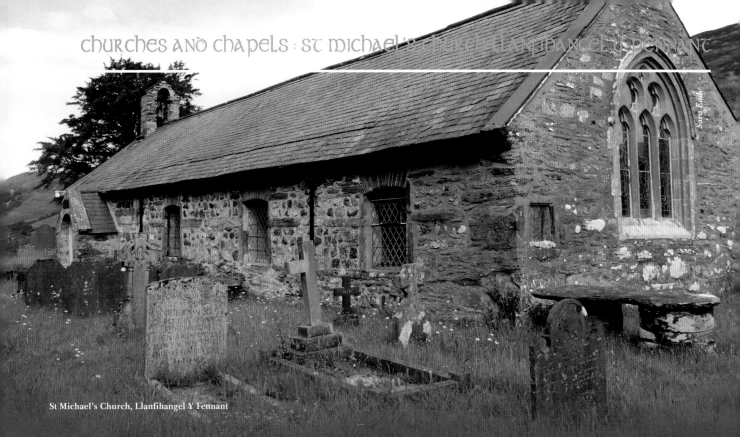

St Michael's Church, Llanfihangel Y Fennant

The Church

St Michael's Church is situated at the foot of Cader Idris and close to Castell y Bere

The current St Michael's Church at Llanfihangel y Pennant is believed to be the third such place of worship in the area with the same name. The first was a small building, built of local slatey stone from the neighbourhood and was unmortared. It was probably built by the people who lived in the area and is now in ruins. It was situated about half a mile from the current site, on the upper slope of Tyn y Fach and it was known as Eglwys Mihangel. The building measured 24ft by

16ft 3ins and lay east to west and was abandoned when Castell y Bere was built. Only a small portion of the walling still exists.

Some 200 yards to the north-west is a similar enclosure formed of rough masonry and measuring about 6ft by 3ft and 2ft deep which is known as Parson's Well and was probably associated with the church. The well is now dry.

Incorporated into Castell y Bere was a chapel called St Michael. When the castle was destroyed a new church was built on the current site in the 13th century.

Porch

The new building, again built of local stone was built in the style of an extended Welsh Longhouse. It was made larger at some stage and the Porch and Vestry were added at a later date. The website, www.churchplansonline, has a plan of the church but which is not like the layout of

Window above the altar

the church today. Further investigation reveals that the plan may have been drawn to obtain a grant for work to be undertaken. The Architect was Henry Edward Kennedy (1840-1897) of Bangor and the plan was dated 1878-1881. This plan shows the porch and the vestry on the same side whereas the layout today has the porch on one side and the vestry on the other.

The church is composed of a nave and chancel with no structural distinction between them, vestry, south porch and western bell gable. The disproportionally large vestry has an original Perpendicular Window, but its opening to the church is square in shape.

In the vestry is a small exhibition commemorating the life of Mary Jones, which includes a Quilt made by Sara Eade, Irene Hale and Pauline Hey in 2006. The Quilt shows an elderly Mary Jones looking back over her life.

Bell Tower

Font

The Font

The font is believed to have come from Castell-y-Bere, the ruins of which can be seen less than half a mile away. The Castle was built between 1120 and 1230 by Llewelyn the Great and was the last castle to fall in the war for Wales.

The Font is made of granite and for the time was very nicely decorated with a series of carved semi-circles. It has a square base and top linked with a circular column. The font is lined with a lead basin and water has to be added for a Christening and then excess water bailed out.

Mary Jones was baptised in this church on the 19th December 1784 following her birth on the 16th December. She and her family attended this church for services on a regular basis. Her father, Jacob, died on the 16th April 1789 when Mary was just 4 years and 4 months old. He is buried in the churchyard to the right as you leave the church.

The Lepers' Window

The window, next to the door into the Vestry at St Michael's Church, Llanfihangel y Pennant is unusual in that it is set in the wall at an angle and is known as the Lepers' Window. It is the only window in the church set at an angle. If you go outside the church and look through the window, you will see the pulpit and when there was a service being taken, the Preacher delivering the sermon would be visible to anyone looking through the window.

In times gone by, those people suffering from leprosy were not allowed to enter the church. Leprosy was considered to be very contagious and people were afraid that if they came into contact with someone who had leprosy, then they would catch it. Whilst leprosy was infectious, it was very difficult to catch and thankfully, today it is curable.

The disease mainly affects the skin, the peripheral nerves, mucosa of the upper respiratory tract and also the eyes, apart from some other structures. Since ancient

Lepers' window

times, leprosy has been regarded, by communities, as a contagious, mutilating and incurable disease.

The window allowed the people with leprosy to take part in a church service without coming into contact with people who did not have the disease.

Thankfully leprosy is very rare in the UK today. There are many countries in Asia, Africa and Latin America with a significant number of leprosy cases. It is estimated that today, there are between one and two million people visibly and irreversibly disabled due to past and present outbreaks of leprosy and who require to be cared for by the community in which they live.

There are a number of organisations working to support people with leprosy and the communities within which they live. Amongst these are The Leprosy Mission and LEPRA.

Mary Jones' quilt

View inside the church from the Lepers' window

Sara Eade

Original Calvanistic Methodist Chapel in Cwrt & the one which Mary would have attended

The Calvinistic Methodist Chapel at Cwrt was erected in 1806 but in the beginning was not used exclusively as a place of worship. The Religious Census of 1851 recorded that the attendances were, Morning – 41 scholars, afternoon – 104 and evening – 63. The Elder, of the Chapel at that time was John Vaughan of Maesllan near Dolgelly.

The Chapel was used until the congregation outgrew it and a larger chapel, called Jerusalem, was built on the opposite side of the river.

The Chapel at Cwrt was later converted into holiday cottages.

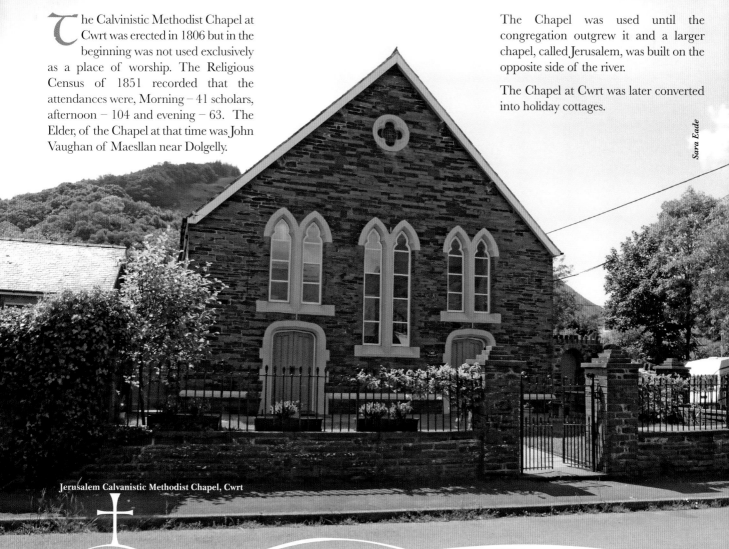

Sara Eade

Jerusalem Calvanistic Methodist Chapel, Cwrt

The Royal Commission on the Ancient and Historical Monuments of Wales records the following about Sardis Chapel:

'Built in 1820 with repairs and alterations carried out in 1939. The Chapel is built in the Vernacular style with a long wall entry plan. Internally a late 19th Century refit appears to have moved the pulpit to the gable end.

The entrance is via the right hand end door on the South-West side. Adjacent to this, on the left, is a now blocked former doorway. The Chapel is lit by one window in each long wall, near the North-West pulpit end of the building. They are earlier 20th Century metal framed replacement windows. Inside, there are limited rafters above a partly extant flat plaster ceiling and there is a painted arch on the pulpit wall and later 19th Century wood fittings including 2

Window in back wall of Sardis

blocks of seats arranged either side of a central aisle, and the pulpit. The chapel closed around 1980 and in 2003 it was still disused with its sale under discussion. The attached row of two roofless stone cottages are up for sale at the same time.'

A Religious Survey undertaken in 1851 recorded the attendance at Sardis as being 69 in the morning and 65 in the evening.

The chapel closed at the end of 1988 and one of the members of the congregation, at that time, was Buddug Thompson. She and her husband Hugh and son Emrys

The main body of the chapel in 2014

were then living at Gernos, a farm within a short walking distance of Mary Jones's home at Tyn y Ddol. The family were moving to Abergynolwyn after 30 years at Gernos. By this time the chapel had only one service on a Sunday and the congregation was down to around 12 people. On leaving the Chapel, the Deacons, Hugh Lloyd Williams and J Morgan Lewis wrote a letter for Buddug so that she could transfer her membership to another Independent Chapel.

The licence for marriages at Sardis was cancelled in 2000.

The Independent churches were ones in which each congregation were autonomous upholding the principles of independence. In the 19th Century they became known as Congregational.

In 1972 the Congregational Church joined with the English Presbyterian Church to become the United Reformed Church. Some Congregational Churches though did not take this path and became members of the Congregational Federation.

Llanfihangel y Pennant, at that time, comprised 8,321 acres with a population of 159 males and 181 females, a total of 376 people.

Letter given to Buddug Thompson

Remains of the cottage next to Sardis in 2014

1 MARY'S RETURN HOME

Almost all of the stories written about Mary Jones and her walk to Bala record that when she returned home, she showed the Bible to her father. Mary walked to Bala in 1800 but her father had died on the 16th April 1789 when Mary was aged just 4 years and 4 months.

2 LYDIA WILLIAMS

In many of the histories written about Mary Jones, Lydia Williams is described as Mary's niece. As far as we know, Mary was an only child and so Lydia could not have been a niece. However in those days, a god-daughter was sometimes referred to as a niece and older women who were close family friends but not relatives were sometimes referred to as Aunts and so Lydia may have been the daughter of such a lady.

3 THE WEIGHT OF THE BIBLES AND WAS MARY ABLE TO CARRY THREE

Some accounts of Mary's walk refer to one Bible, some two and some three. Mary herself sometimes said two and sometimes three but could she have carried three if there were three? The Bible that Mary brought back for her Aunt, Ann Richards weighs 1258 grams (approximately 2lb 3ozs) so the weight of three would be 3774 grams (approximately 6lb 9 ozs).

Almost all of the stories talk about Mary having a wallet which she carried over her shoulder and on the journey to Bala had her clogs in one end and food for the journey in the other end. The Wallet was made from a long length of fabric which was enclosed at both ends and also along both sides but leaving a gap in the middle of one side which would have been at the point where the Wallet went over her shoulder.

On the return journey Mary would probably have had two Bibles at one end and the third and her clogs at the other end thus balancing the weight nicely.

The Bible given to Ann Richards measures 5¼ inches across the top, 8¼ inches down the side and is 3¼ inches thick.

4 WHEN DID MARY UNDERTAKE THE WALK TO BALA

The Rev David E Jenkins when he wrote his 'Life of Thomas Charles' had access to Thomas' diaries and letters and suggest from the evidence he had seen, that Mary made the walk in early September 1800. The Bibles printed in 1799 did not leave London until May 1800.

5 WERE ALL THE BIBLES OBTAINED AT THE SAME TIME

The two Bibles that are available to view certainly were printed in the same year MDCCXCIX – 1799 and both were printed by W Dawson, T Bensley and A J Cooke of the Clarendon Printing House. The current location of the third Bible is unknown. The Rev David Jenkins suggests that a third Bible has the name Margaret Jones in it. I am of the opinion that Mary may have given the third Bible to her son John when he emigrated to America.

6 THE OWNER OF THE SECOND BIBLE

Some research must have been untaken in 1885 as a copy of a letter exists written by Elizabeth Jones, wife of Griffith Jones of Gwyddfynyd Farm, Bryncrug, on the 26th October:

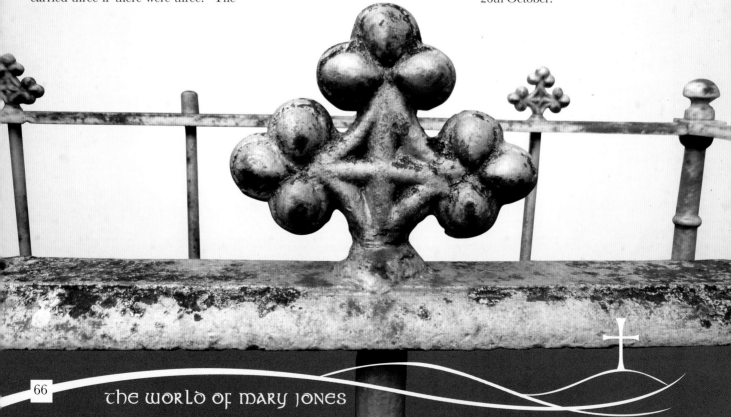

'Dear Friend

In answer to your letter I beg to give you all the information I have been able to get concerning the other Bible Mary Jones brought from Bala.

She brought it for her Aunt, cousin to her mother named Anne Richard, Tynyr eithiw near Bryncrug, where she died. At her death her son had it who had married a daughter of the old preacher William Pugh Cwrt Abergynolwyn. Their daughter Lydia Williams lived at Bryncrug and I saw the bible in her possession. She gave it to our governess Miss Jones now Mrs Rowlands, Board School Penrhyndeudraeth, who has it still at least had it when I saw her last. It has been no trouble at all to me to gain this information. Should you require any other information I shall be glad to help you.

With best respects

Yours truly

Elizabeth Jones'

Lizzie Rowlands passed the Bible to Robert Oliver Rees to restore it as by now it was in need of repair and with the instruction that it should then be presented to the College at Bala. This however, didn't happen straight away and when, some five years later, Lizzie went to tea with Mrs Edwards, wife of Dr Lewis Edwards, at the College, she discovered that the Bible had not been deposited in the library as she had requested. Lizzie followed this up and the bible finally made its way to the college. It was later deposited in the National Library of Wales at Aberystwyth, where it can be seen today.

All the illustrations in this section are from the gravestone of Mary Jones in the graveyard at Bryncrug.

7 how much influence did mary jones' walk to bala have on rev thomas charles

The answer to this question would be easy if Thomas had mentioned Mary's walk to Bala to buy a Bible in his diary but he didn't. The only clue we get is in a letter that Thomas wrote to Joseph Tarn in a reply to a letter which Joseph had written to Thomas on the 7th March 1804 from London:

'Young females, in service, have walked over thirty miles to me with only the bare hope of obtaining a Bible each; and returned with more joy and thanksgiving than if they had obtained great spoils. We, who have half a dozen Bibles by us, and are in circumstances to obtain as many more, know but little of the value those put upon one, who before were hardly permitted to look into a Bible once a week.'

Whilst today, Mary Jones and the start of the British and Foreign Bible Society are seen as very heavily connected, the reality is that it was only after 1862, that the connection has been promoted.

8 the cost of the bible

We know that Mary brought three Bibles back with her from Bala and that she saved 3s and 6d, herself, for the cost of her bible. We also know that she brought a Bible back for her Aunt, Ann Richards, which presumably was paid for by her Aunt. The third Bible was given to her by Rev Thomas Charles as a gift. The cost of Bibles in London, at that time, was 2s 9d and the cost of carriage for a Bible from London to Bala was 9d, thus making the cost of 3s 6d.

The Rev Thomas Charles, with thanks to the generosity of his many friends who made it possible for him to give Bibles to people at no cost, was able to give Bibles away, free of any charge. In effect Mary had a free Bible, which in turn she may have given away or she may have sold when she returned – we will probably never know

9 mary or mari

In none of the official records, births, marriages or death registers, is Mary referred to as Mari. Lizzie Rowlands always calls her Mary as does other material relating to Mary and written while she was alive.

Some of the many books written about Mary Jones

Cover of the book by Robert Oliver Rees

Sara Eade Collection

The controversial picture of Mary Jones

Sara Eade Collection

Robert was baptised on the 22nd May 1818 in Dolgelley, the son of Ellis Rees and Catherine and he was one of five children. His father was a Victualler by trade but he had also been a Butcher, a Banker's Clerk and an Inn Keeper.

Robert trained to be a Druggist and he was also a Bookseller. In the 1851 and 1861 censuses Robert was living in Eldon Square, Dolgelley and in 1871 he was living in Lion Street in Dolgelley.

Robert never married and died on the 12th February 1881 in Dolgelley and he was aged 62. He left a Will with an estate of under £600. Probate was granted to his sisters, Jane Williams, Margaret Morgans and Elizabeth Roberts.

When Lizzie Rowlands read Robert's account of Mary Jones and her journey to obtain a Welsh Bible, she was quite upset as she felt that he had got several things wrong and that the illustration he had used was really nothing like Mary at all. She wrote to Robert pointing out the inaccuracies!

Cover of the book by Mary E Roper

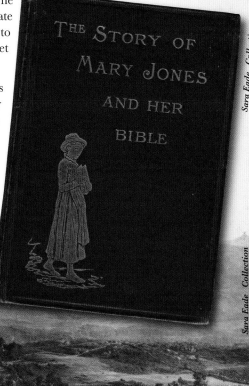

Sara Eade Collection

Whilst Robert Oliver Rees was not known to Mary Jones, as far as we know, he was the man who first wrote her story which was first published in 1878 some fourteen years after her death. The book was in Welsh and entitled 'Mary Jones a sefydliad Y Beibl Gymdeithas'. This book was later translated into English and was entitled 'The Story of Mary Jones and her Bible' by M E R (Mary E Roper) in 1882.

Dolgelley and Cader Idris

Sara Eade Collection

Sara Eade

St Michael's Church, Llanfihangel y Pennant

Curate of Llanfihangel y Pennant and Talyllyn Churches in the 1790s

The Rev William Pugh was educated at Jesus College, Oxford and in 1774, after four years, obtained a BA (Bachelor of Arts degree) and on the 29th May 1774 he was ordained a Deacon by Bishop Shute of Bangor, at Christ Church, Oxford. Two years later on the 22nd September 1776, he was ordained a Priest at Bangor Cathedral again by Bishop Shute. William then spent time at Llandanwg and Llanfair, near to Harlech in Merionethshire before marrying Mary Jones on the 18th April 1777 and shortly after became a Priest at Dolgellau.

William and Mary had ten children; Hugh baptised at Llanfair on the 23rd May 1778, Jane baptised at Llanfair on the 18th April 1780, Catherine, baptised on the 8th November 1782, John Richard, baptised at Llanfair on the 6th April 1785, William, baptised at Llanfair on the 11th November 1787, Lowry baptised on the 22nd March 1789, William baptised on the 23rd October 1791, Richard baptised on the 9th August 1793, David baptised on the 12th July 1795, Sara baptised on the 17th June 1797 and Catherine baptised on the 17th January 1800 at Llanfair. The first Catherine and William along with Richard, David and Sara all died young.

Sara Eade

View of the Church from the Pulpit

Sara Eade

One of the oldest grave stones dated 1691

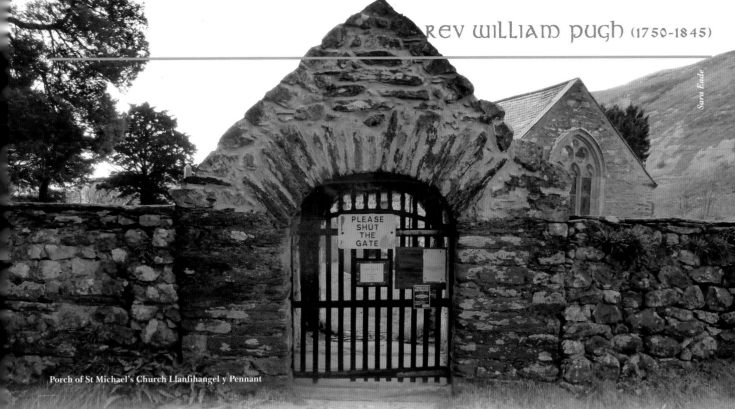

Porch of St Michael's Church Llanfihangel y Pennant

Whilst at Llanfihangel y Pennant, William shocked his neighbours by shooting one of his parishioners, William Lewis Owen on the 17th March 1796. An account of this event is contained in *From Merioneth to Botany Bay* by Hugh J Owen in a chapter entitled *The Fiery Cleric*:

'Owen died of his wounds three days afterwards. This fiery cleric was arrested and charged with manslaughter at the Merioneth Court of Great Sessions held at Bala. In the words of the indictment he was said not to have the fear of God before his eyes but was moved and seduced by the instigation of the devil.

From the brief particulars of the charge contained in the Indictment, the Reverend William Pugh loaded and charged his gun "with gunpowder and a little brown paper" and shot Owen in the shoulder.

Perhaps an explanation should be given of the description "gunpowder and a little brown paper". The gun of the period was a flintlock. The gun was loaded by pouring the powder down the muzzle, then ramming down a wad and then the bullet. On pulling the trigger, the flint caused a spark which ignited the powder and fired the bullet.

From the words of the Indictment it would appear that in this particular case a wad of paper only was rammed down the barrel. If fired at anyone, point blank, at a vital spot, it might kill. In this case, however, Owen was only shot in the shoulder, but even this proved fatal.

This cleric was found "Not Guilty", but there is nothing in the records to suggest the reasons which prompted the jury to come to that conclusion.

There must, however, have been some exceptional features in the case to have justified the acquittal of the accused. The case against the cleric could not have been so bad as he was allowed to remain in his living; further, on the 7th May 1801, he was instituted as Curate at Llanfair with Harlech, and on the 13th February 1816, was appointed Vicar of that living.'

William remained at Llanfair until his death in 1845 at the age of ninety-five years.

It is thought that Lowry Pugh, the sixth child of William and Mary, married a Lewis Williams, a School Master at Abergynolwyn, and that their daughter Lydia was the lady who lived with Mary Jones at her cottage in Bryncrug. Lydia was certainly living with Mary Jones in 1861 as the census lists her aged 46 and Mary as aged 76.

The place coffins were rested

A YOUNG GIRL'S DREAM *by Irene Hale*

As I awake this morning,
To a new day dawning,
All around I see
Majestic mountains looking back at me.
For the vision I see one day
A Bible will belong to me.

I am of Weaver's stock,
The work is hard,
The pay is poor.
Ours is just a humble abode,
Where love for each other grows
A home where Bible stories are told.

Throughout my childhood,
I have saved my money,
Doing errands around the village
Selling eggs and honey.

Now I am sixteen,
All those childhood aspirations
I had so long ago,
Barefoot to Bala I now must go.
Across the mountain track,
I meet a man upon a white horse,
Who directed me to Bala,
To the Rev Thomas Charles' door.

My heart is beating fast,
For a Bible is within my grasp.
As the door opens, It is the man I saw
Upon the white horse.
Rev Thomas Charles, he sold me a Welsh written Bible
That I hold so close to my heart.

David Hale

The *Cambrian News and Merionethshire Standard* carried the following report on the 7th June 1907:

'Unveiling of Mrs Mary Jones's Memorial

Last Saturday, in the premises of a large concourse of people, the memorial stone to Mrs Mary Jones of Tynyddol, Llanfihangel y Pennant, was unveiled at that place by Miss Annie Daniel, Brynhyfryd, Towyn. The monument has been erected on the site of the old dwelling place of Mrs Mary Jones and is enclosed by a stone wall. About half past two in the afternoon the Rev Madoc Roberts (W), Towyn commenced the proceedings by reading a portion of Scripture and engaging in prayer. The president in his inaugural address said that he was in London the week before and went to see Mary Jones's Bible which is being kept in the Office of the Bible Society. Mrs Mary Jones walked all the way from Llanfihangel to Bala a distance of twenty miles to ask for a copy of the Bible from the Rev Thomas Charles and this act of hers had immortalised her name. She walked back and brought with her the greatest treasure of her life, a copy of the Bible. The Rev Humphrey Williams, one of the secretaries of the movement was called upon to read the correspondence. Letters from the following expressing regret at their inability to attend were read:- M E Thomas Tynyberth, Corris, the Rev J M Williams, Towyn, the Rev D R Pugh MA, vicar, Towyn, and Rev D Charles Edward. Miss Annie Daniel then unveiled the monument and read the following inscription which it bore:- "In memory of Mari Jones, who in the year 1800, when 16 years of age, walked from this place to Bala to get a Bible from the Rev Thomas Charles, BA. This occurrence was the cause of the establishment of the British and Foreign Bible Society." The Rev R C Evans (A) Abergynolwyn delivered a short address and so did the Rev R Jones, Abergynolwyn and Mr Hugh Pugh, Llanegryn. The Rev R R Williams, MA, observed that what was being done that day was the consummation of persevering work of years and it was Miss Annie Daniel who first started the work and had remained faithful to it to the end. It was the penny offertory of the Sunday School scholars that enabled miss Daniel to complete the work. It was announced that Mr Griffith, the owner of Tynyddol, the old residence of Mari Jones, had conveyed the place as a freehold inheritance to the Committee. After singing a hymn, the meeting was closed by Councillor Maethlon James offering up a prayer.'

Margaret Lloyd Rees Collection